To our

[illegible]

Faith

We love you!
You are an inspiration
and an example
to us.
Robert + Rosalie

Dr. Robert Owens

Robert R. Owens
2021

ISBN: 9781795353229

Cover Art and Design by: Dr. Robert Owens

Table of Contents

Introduction

Faith

All it takes is faith to be saved, to be born-again, to become right with God, to become His child, to have the ability to stand in His presence without the sense of any guilt, or shame, or condemnation. All we need to do is confess with our mouth the Lord Jesus. In other words accept Him and proclaim Him as the leader of our life and believe in our heart that God raised Him from the dead and we will be saved.[1] That's it. Just confess and believe.

But what is this faith that we're talking about?

The fundamental fact of existence is that this trust in God, this faith, is the firm foundation under everything that makes life worth living. It's our handle on what we can't see.[2]

---

[1] Bible Gateway https://www.biblegateway.com/passage/?search=romans+10%3A9&version=NKJV 1-26-19

[2] Bible Gateway https://www.biblegateway.com/passage/?search=hebrews+11%3A1-How does this faith relate to the world around us?2&version=MSG 1-26-19

By faith we understand that the worlds were framed by the word of God, so that the things which are seen were not made of things which are visible. Instead the very substance of creation is faith. It isn't some sort of add-on meant to enhance our existence; instead it's the source and the summit of all that exists.[3]

It was God's faith in His own Word when He said, "Let there be," that created all things.[4] And it's His faith that keeps existence existing.

Without faith it's impossible to please Him, for he who comes to God must believe that He is, and that He rewards those who diligently seek Him.[5]

We can follow all the traditions and fulfill all the ceremonies of any religion we chose, but if we don't have faith in Christ and His resurrection we're wasting our time. We're spinning wheels going nowhere, dust in the wind, flowers that bloom for a moment and are gone. But with faith in Christ and His resurrection we've already entered into eternal life. Once we open ourselves to

---

[3] Bible Gateway https://www.biblegateway.com/passage/?search=hebrews+11%3A3&version=NKJV 1-26-19

[4] Bible Gateway https://www.biblegateway.com/passage/?search=genisis+1&version=NKJV 1-26-19

[5] Bible Gateway https://www.biblegateway.com/passage/?search=hebrews+11%3A6&version=NKJV 1-26-19

Christ and die to self we've done all the dying we'll ever do. Our bodies will surely assume room temperature someday but we'll live forever united with Christ in the throne room of God.

In the following pages I reflect on some thoughts about God and how walking through this world hand-in-hand with Him helps us not only cope but overcome.[6] I try to share my faith. For our witness is all we really have to share that is of eternal significance. This is our calling. For just as He told Paul He also tells us, "For you will be His witness to all men of what you have seen and heard."[7,8] For just like Paul, we were blind and we couldn't see but now through faith in Christ who is the light of the world we can walk in the light.[9,10]

This whole living a life of faith is expressed as well as it ever could be by Eugene Peterson in *The Message*,[11] "What actually took place

---

[6] Bible Gateway https://www.biblegateway.com/passage/?search=1+john+5%3A4&version=NKJV 1-26-19

[7] Bible Gateway https://www.biblegateway.com/passage/?search=acts+22%3A10-15&version=NKJV 1-26-19

[8] Bible Gateway https://www.biblegateway.com/passage/?search=acts+1%3A8&version=NKJV 1-27-19

[9] Bible Gateway https://www.biblegateway.com/passage/?search=Psalm+56%3A13&version=NKJV 1-26-19

[10] Bible Gateway https://www.biblegateway.com/passage/?search=john+12%3A46&version=NKJV 1-27-19

[11] The Message http://messagebible.com/ 1-27-19

is this: I tried keeping rules and working my head off to please God, and it didn't work. So I quit being a "law man" so that I could be God's man. Christ's life showed me how, and enabled me to do it. I identified myself completely with him. Indeed, I have been crucified with Christ. My ego is no longer central. It is no longer important that I appear righteous before you or have your good opinion, and I am no longer driven to impress God. Christ lives in me. The life you see me living is not mine, but it is lived by faith in the Son of God, who loved me and gave himself for me. I am not going to go back on that."[12]

All I can say to that is: Amen and Amen.

Robert R. Owens

---

[12] Bible Gateway https://www.biblegateway.com/passage/?search=galatians+2%3A20&version=MSG 1-26-19

Reflection One

A Childless Father Who Has a Son

I am blessed. My wife gave me a son. He was hers before he was mine. Then he became ours. In my heart he is always mine and I feel as if I am his Dad. But it often feels like a homerun record with an asterisk, an almost. You see, I'm a step-father. That's as close as I will ever come to experiencing the life of a father and for that I am forever thankful to God for I am a childless father who has a son.

I know the pride of watching my son play little league. Together we experienced the joy of victory and the agony of defeat. I encouraged him to play music. I helped with homework. I watched him march in band. I raced against the stop lights time after time to make it to events and meetings with teachers, doctor's appointments, and birthdays. I watched him graduate grade school after driving him from one town to another so he could remain in the same school with his friends after we moved. I blessed God when he graduated high school and earned scholarships to college. I was happy when he chose the girl my wife and I prayed for long before we ever met her, enjoyed being the father of the groom, and I love my grandchildren with all my heart. I am truly blessed. My wife gave me a son.

But there are four other children I have never known. Four other children blood of my blood and bone of my bone that I never had the chance to know.

These are my aborted children.

They were aborted without my consent, told by the women involved and the courts that it was none of my business, murdered within the law, slaughtered beyond the pale. They are still alive within my heart.

Let me say in defense of the women who aborted my children, before I gave my life to Christ I was a snake. As a matter of fact I've always said that before I was saved snakes would cross the street when they saw me coming. I was a drug addicted; drunken scheming dreamer convinced I should be something I wasn't and equally convince I wasn't what I was.

Any young woman who learned they were pregnant and that I was the father could not be blamed for deciding I was a waste of space, a self-indulgent loser, and a disaster as a potential father. And although none of the three young women involved ever told me why they aborted my children, that's what I have always thought was my addition to the equation.

Once I gave my life to Christ. Once I sobered up, straightened out, and stood in the light of His love I knew he forgave me for any part I played in the deaths of these innocent children. I know He forgives everyone who lays their sins at the foot of the cross.

Over the years He has ministered to my heart, my spirit, and my soul as I have cried tears for who could have been. I am healed for when He said, "It is finished," sin was defeated. When He rose from the grave life conquered death, and since He ascended into heaven where He took His place at the right hand of the Father together we all live in Him. I am healed.

But there is not a day I don't miss those children. There is not a day I don't think of what might have been. There is not a day that I don't imagine seeing them in Him.

I struggle sometimes knowing that two of the women who aborted my children later had other children. They've had an experience they took from me. I don't begrudge them the joy of parenting. I have forgiven them. But sometimes I'm jealous of what they have and of what I shall never have and for this I repent. I also struggle sometimes watching other women I know have had abortions and later had children. I know God has forgiven them. I don't have anything against them but at times I struggle with my own emotions.

All of this is the burden of this forgotten father. I was forgotten in the decision to abort my children. I have been forgotten in all the years since.

I may be forgotten but I cannot forget.

My children died. Four lost lives in the American holocaust of millions. They are four souls whose blood cries out to God, four cracks in my broken heart, four children of God I long to know, four tears I shall cry till the day we meet.

A step-father is like a used shoe. It may look good, it may wear well, and at time it may even feel good. But it's still a used shoe.

However my step-son may feel about me I know how I feel about him. He is my son. I may have lost four but I have gained one. I am blessed. My wife gave me a son.

Reflection Two

A New You for a New Year

Are you sick and tired of being sick and tired? Have you reached the end of your rope only to find out that it's much shorter than you imagined? Was last year as good as you hoped it would be? Was it as bad as you feared it would be? Does the uncertainty of the future leave you anxious? Has your own mortality entered like a crack in the ice of your youthful belief in personal indestructability?

But wait there's more...

Does the randomness of good happening to bad people and bad happening to good people leave you wondering if there's any rhyme or reason to reality? Is looking for answers to these and many other questions like looking for needles in haystacks? Is the quest to find meaning in life like trying to nail fog to the wall?

If you've rejected Christ because of Christians don't mistake the messengers for the message. Christ told his followers to lake His light to the world and most have spent the last 2018 years trying to build a lamp and pretending it was the light.

The message is as simple as receiving it: Confess Jesus as Lord and believe in your heart that God raised him from the dead and you will be saved.

That's it.

It's not about joining the right club or following the right rules. We don't need a seminary degree or someone with one to walk us through learning the secret handshake or the Abra Kadabra password. And there is no magic decoder ring. We don't have to read the Bible from cover to cover. We don't have to wear the right clothes, beard, or haircut. We don't have to vote for the right candidates. We don't have to take an oath to believe the same things that everyone else who confesses Christ as Lord does.

It isn't about being good enough. That's one of the great miracles of God's economy. While we were yet sinners Jesus came and died so that we could live.

It isn't about becoming a religious robot who says the right things at the right time to the right people in the right place. God is the One who created us with free choice, so we're free to choose. It isn't about conformity. God is the One who created us to be an individual and He doesn't make junk. We are who He created us to be. He has placed us in a certain time and place so that we can become all He designed us to be and do all that He has called us to do. And that means what He created, placed, and called you to be will be different than what He created, placed, and called me to be. You see it isn't about cookie-cutter, repeat a formula, and follow the rule book club membership.

It's about each of us individually confessing Jesus as Lord and each of us individually believing God raised Jesus from the dead and then learning to commune with God, to hear Him speak to us as individuals and then doing what He tells us to do.

If the questions at the beginning of this article float through our minds like storm clouds in a cloudless sky obscuring what should be clear. Let's give up the battle to do it on our own. Let's surrender and find victory in allowing God to count the victory of Jesus over sin and death to our account.

It's so easy we can do it right here right now. We don't need to be in a meeting, at an altar, or in a special building. We don't need anyone to hold our hand or even know what we've done. We will know. God will know. And once we're in his hand no one can snatch us out.

I confess Jesus as Lord and I believe in my heart that God raised Him from the Dead. That's it. All done. The battle is over. The war between us and God is over and we are one with Him. Welcome to a new you for a new year.

Reflection Three

A Soap Opera That Never Ends
Will Finally End
Then What?

All my life I've been in love with History. I learned at an early age that if you love reading you can live a thousand lifetimes and if you're wise you have the opportunity to learn from the mistakes of others. I've certainly experienced the former while unfortunately not doing much of the latter.

My love of History metastasized into a love of Political Science. These two intellectual "Loves of my Life" have given me countless hours of joy lost in reading, mired in thinking, and entertained by speculation.

Now as I enter what are called the golden years, though I believe they might be made of brass, having spent several decades teaching both subjects I feel a need to share some insights not on particulars but instead on something that is usually disparaged and often dismissed, generalities.

Though most have never heard of him many can misquote the writer and philosopher

George Santayana who is reported to have said, "Those who do not learn history are doomed to repeat it." What he actually said was, "Those who cannot remember the past are condemned to repeat it." There is a subtle difference there for learning and remembering are two different things. This sounds so wise. It even appears self-evident. And it apparently, at least to my observation, it's an oxymoron. After a daily study of History for sixty years the only lesson I've learned is that humanity never learns the lessons of History.

In my classes I tell my students that History is nothing more than the stories of people just like us who lived at different times in what were essentially different worlds. They had the same bodies and minds that we do. They felt the same emotions. They lived, they died, and now it is our turn. I also tell them that if we don't learn anything from History that helps us in our everyday life we might as well read fiction.

I know that most people study History because they have to. I know most people find it boring. As an exercise in memorizing dates, names, and facts to be later regurgitated on a test and forgotten I can well understand the boring part. There are so few who can see through to the stories making History so exciting. So few can lose themselves in the narrative, imagine themselves on the deck of that ship, in the palace with the king, or in the hut with that peasant. They only see dates, and names, and facts. BORING!

And Political Science who cares about that? I tell my students who don't care about it at all that it's the science of who gets what and if they don't care about it someone else will and then they get to make the decisions. So what do you want? You decide.

Now after decades spent following politics through the lens of History attempting to share with others the insights gained I must tell you all that it's essentially the equivalent of an ant studying a castle made of sand. He spends his life telling other ants how wondrous the castle is, how imposing its turrets are, how deep its moat, and how formidable its defenses then the waves come in the castle is gone and the ants have disappeared.

I recently taught a class on American History from 1877 until the present to a class full of millennials. We used a textbook that was more than a thousand pages long. It wasn't until the last few pages that we reached anything the students could remember as having happened since they became aware of the world around them. That last twenty minutes of the semester really had an impact.

To most people History begins the day they're born. For all of us it ends the day we die. And Political Science ends up being the science of rearranging the deck chairs on the Titanic.

In the 4.5 billion years of this planets existence, in the fifteen billion years since the Big Bang the history of humanity doesn't even take up the last few pages. It would fill perhaps part of a sentence, a few words such as............... All things will pass only those things done in Christ will last.

That's it. The sum total of all I have learned, all I have discovered, and all I will ever know. No Christ no peace. Know Crist know peace. For those who seek to gain their life will lose it and those who lose their life for Christ will find it. He is the truth, the light, and the life and without Him there is no truth, or light, or life.

Stop fighting a war that's already been won. Stop spinning your wheels running in a race that goes in a circle. Step out of the darkness and into the light and let this be the first day of the rest of your life.

The stories of those who have gone before teach us nothing if they don't lead us to Christ. The politics of this world are an endless loop, a tempest in a teacup, a soap opera that never ends. It may be engaging to watch like a slow motion train wreck. It may be exciting, exhilarating, even entertaining but for most of us in a hundred years no one will even know we were here. In a thousand years no one will remember the compelling arguments of today, the all-important bitter debates about whether we place the deck chair here or there. Yet in an eternity from now heaven will know whether or not we acknowledged Christ as our Savior, for if we confess with our lips that Jesus is Lord and believe in our hearts that God raised Him from the dead we shall be saved.

Reflection Four

Choose This Day Who You Will Serve

In our current confrontation with Radical Islam the battle lines are portrayed as those between a secular society, us and a religious society, them. I reject this portrayal as a betrayal of the faith of our Founders and of those patriotic Americans who still hold fast to Jesus as God and Savior, we too are a religious people.

America was founded as a Christian country. Anyone who denies that has not studied enough History or has been sadly misled. Columbus accentuated his desire to spread the Christian faith to his patrons the King and Queen of Spain and in his log. The first thing the English did upon landing at Jamestown was set up a cross to dedicate their endeavor to Jesus their Savior. Were these early explorers and colonists always true to their faith? Did they always operate under principles derived from God's Word? Sadly they did not. However, to say that the Christian faith was not an integral part of their motivation and worldview is simply not true.

In the latter part of the twentieth century Progressive leaders pushing a collectivist agenda decided to declare us a pluralistic society.[13] They sought to detach the heavily Bible influenced Constitution into the dustbin of History by substituting what they call a living constitution for the rock-solid one the Framers bequeathed us. Mr. Obama, the quintessential Progressive in his speech to the Muslims of Egypt, Turkey, and many places spiced up his apology tours[14] by asserting that America is not a Christian country.[15] This statement of his belief and goal does not make it true.

All of these recent changes aside, most Americans still believe in God[16] and the majority[17] continues to consider themselves Christians. As a Christian, an Historian, and a Political Scientist in response to numerous questions I would like to share my beliefs concerning government, economies, and the rights of man.

As far as a government goes the only Biblically correct one is that God is God and

---

[13] Answers http://www.answers.com/Q/What_is_a_Pluralistic_society 1-24-19

[14] You Tube https://www.youtube.com/watch?v=DAXA0WVwxiE 1-24-19

[15] You Tube https://www.youtube.com/watch?v=tmC3IevZiik 1-24-19

[16] Gallup https://news.gallup.com/poll/147887/americans-continue-believe-god.aspx 1-24-19

[17] Townhall https://townhall.com/tipsheet/brandonross/2018/04/27/untitled-n2475435 1-24-19

we are His people. He is the King and we are the sheep of His pasture. As concerning an economic system God's economy knows no lack and is exceedingly abundantly provisioned by the owner of the cattle on a thousand hills.

This being true I do not believe that God mandates any type of human government or economic system as pre-ordained, sanctified, or holy. However, I do believe that humanity as God has created it does require certain governmental and economic conditions to develop and thrive as God intended.

God created us in His own image.[18] He gave us the power to create and to choose.[19] He gave us a mind open to learning and ever eager to improvise. He also gave us what I believe is the most crucial aspect of our make-up: our free will or the power to choose. We can choose to follow Him and do what He desires, or we can choose to follow the leadings not only of our thoughts but of our emotions also. In other words we can dwell within the Kingdom of God wherein He is our King and we are His people or we can choose to live in the Kingdom of man and become the subjects of either our own

---

[18] Bible Gateway https://www.biblegateway.com/passage/?search=Genesis+1%3A27&version=NKJV 1-24-19

[19] Bible Gateway https://www.biblegateway.com/passage/?search=Joshua+24%3A15&version=NKJV 1-24-19

designs or of whoever manages to gain control of the physical world around us.

If God wanted slaves or robots He could have created slaves or robots. Instead He created us and gave us a mind to think and a will to choose because He wanted us to decide to love Him and follow Him freely without compulsion. Therefore I believe that since free thought and free choice are the foundation of man's nature freedom is necessary if man is to live as God designed. This being the case I believe that any governmental or economic system that denies man's freedom interferes with and attempts to supplant God's plan, which is the definition of evil.

There are of course limits to freedom as expressed in the Ten Commandments. Beyond this we should be free to choose our own way. Will we follow God or will we follow man. Within these limits and building on the moral framework the Bible provides I believe that a republic based upon the commitment to life, liberty, and the pursuit of happiness using democratic principles is the governmental structure which most closely matches man's God-given nature. I also believe that free market capitalism is the economic system which best allows man to develop and live as God intended. Conversely, when man rejects God and seeks to create his own utopia he builds some sort of centrally-planned command economy and the intrusive government needed to impose it upon others.

A free economy and the free government it requires allows the independent choices of many to produce the greatest prosperity for all as everyone seeks to do the best they can because they reap the rewards. In a socialist or any type of hybrid economy between capitalism and socialism bureaucrats make the decisions and stagnation is the inevitable result. As Gary North, a Christian economist express it, "The essence of democratic socialism is this re-written version of God's commandment: 'Thou shalt not steal, except by majority vote.'"[20] Or as Winston Churchill observed, "Socialism is a philosophy of failure, the creed of ignorance, and the gospel of envy, its inherent virtue is the equal sharing of misery."[21] And that is not life as God intended.

If we look at History it is an outworking of the initial fall of man. In the beginning God created the world including man and it was all good. Then at the dawn of our existence we choose to go our own way instead of following God. We chose to follow the siren

---

[20] Gary North's Specific Answers https://www.garynorth.com/public/department57.cfm 1-24-19

[21] Brainy Quotes https://www.brainyquote.com/quotes/winston_churchill_164131 1-24-19

song of "You shall be like God"[22] and ever since we have attempted to create heaven on earth. All we have succeeded in doing is to open the gates of Hell instead. A case in point would be the age-old question, if God is good why is there evil in the world followed by the age-old answer God gave us free choice and we chose evil.

With the help and guidance of those who seek to play god themselves humanity has often been convinced to surrender their freedom for security, to bargain away their God-given nature and assume the subservient nature of slaves.

In America the purveyors of socialism cloak their designs in the language of populism. They loudly proclaim that they seek a fair deal for everyone, except of course for the people they intend to loot. They want fair elections as long as nothing is done to stop fraudulent voting. They want equality enforced by unequal treatment. In other words they seek to build the kingdom of man where they can be king.

We have a mind to think and the capacity to make a free choice. As the day of reckoning draws near all I can recommend is, think and choose. We can choose to follow the path of redistribution, class warfare, and collectivist

---

[22] Bible Gateway https://www.biblegateway.com/passage/?search=Genesis+3%3A1-4&version=NKJV 1-24-19

dependency or we can choose to at least attempt a return to limited government, personal liberty, and economic freedom. Don't be fooled by the progressive media and their obvious bias. To be free is God's design. For us to be a slave to dependency is man's.

One of America's most beloved troubadours told us, "The words of the prophets are written on the subway walls and tenement halls"[23] and one of those secular prophets he was referring to reminded us "You're gonna have to serve somebody, yes indeed You're gonna have to serve somebody, Well, it may be the devil or it may be the Lord But you're gonna have to serve somebody."[24]

Or as my favorite book says it, "And if it seems evil to you to serve the Lord, choose for yourselves this day whom you will serve, whether the gods which your fathers served that *were* on the other side of the River, or the gods of the Amorites, in whose land you dwell. But as for me and my house, we will serve the Lord."[25]

---

[23] Lyrics Freaks https://www.lyricsfreak.com/p/paul+simon/sounds+of+silence_20559740.html 1-24-19

[24] AZ https://www.azlyrics.com/lyrics/bobdylan/gottaservesomebody.html 1-24-19

[25] Bible Gateway https://www.biblegateway.com/passage/?search=Joshua%2024:15&version=NKJV 1-24-19

Reflection Five

Do You Want To Be Free?

In America today how many laws are there?

The simple answer is no one knows. Does that mean no one can count that high or that they've never been collected into one massive code. Where's Hammurabi or Justinian when you need them?

When the federal laws were first codified in 1927, they fit into a single volume. By the 1980s, there were 50 volumes of more than 23,000 pages. By 2015 it was over 80 volumes and more than 80,000 pages. Today you can't even find out the most recent count using the all-knowing Google. In other words all of us have broken a law somewhere along the line the government just hasn't decided to pick us up yet.

That's sort of how the Mosaic Law is. No one can keep it. Jews couldn't and we can't.

And praise God we don't have to.

The Law of God is called the Mosaic Law. The Mosaic Law consists of the rules of conduct given to Moses by God, as described in the Old Testament. The Mosaic Law begins with the Ten Commandments, but it also includes the rules set forth in the Torah, the first five books of the Old Testament. These codes and the resulting explanation of them in the Talmud enumerate to the nth degree what every Jew should do about everything.

This burden was too heavy for any human to carry which is why Jesus came to fulfill the Law. And that is what He said He came to do, "Do not think that I came to destroy the Law or the Prophets. I did not come to destroy but to fulfill."[26]

He accompanied this statement with a small commentary on the law which spiritualized what the Jews had taken literally.

He said, "You're familiar with the command to the ancients, 'Do not murder.' I'm telling you that anyone who is so much as angry with a brother or sister is guilty of murder." And as if that didn't make it impossible to fulfIll He went even further, "Carelessly call a brother 'idiot!' and you just might find yourself hauled into court. Thoughtlessly yell 'stupid!' at a sister and you are on the brink of hellfire. The simple moral fact is that words kill."

---

[26] Bible Gateway https://www.biblegateway.com/passage/?search=matthew+5%3A17&version=NKJV 1-24-19

Sure we might be able to resist the temptation to murder people but does that mean we've fulfilled the law? No Jesus tells us if we get angry with people, if we call people names we're guilty. Have you ever done that? All I can say is, "Guilty."

If we're going to try to live under the Law we're lost. We're convicted and worthy of nothing but the hellfire of eternal separation from God which sounds like a real drag.

My advice: Don't go there.

The Mosaic Law is like the Federal Law. It's so all-encompassing and so heavy no one can lift it. In other words all of us have broken one of the Mosaic Laws somewhere along the line God just hasn't decided to judge us yet.

My advice: Get out from under the Law.

You might ask, "How are we supposed to do that?"

My advice: Refer to the operator's manual for the planet Earth; the Bible.

Jesus himself gives us the answer. When asked by the super-sized religious folks of His day, "Teacher, which is the great commandment in the law?"[27]

---

[27] Bible Gateway https://www.biblegateway.com/passage/?search=Matthew+22%3A36&version=NKJV 1-24-19

He gave them the answer, "You shall love the Lord your God with all your heart, with all your soul, and with all your mind. This is the first and great commandment. And the second is like it: You shall love your neighbor as yourself. On these two commandments hang all the Law and the Prophets."[28]

That's it. All the rest was for the Jews under the Old Covenant. That deal was completed back when Jesus hung on the cross and said, "After this, Jesus, knowing that all things were now accomplished, that the Scripture might be fulfilled, said, 'I thirst!' Now a vessel full of sour wine was sitting there; and they filled a sponge with sour wine, put it on hyssop, and put it to His mouth. So when Jesus had received the sour wine, He said, 'It is finished!' And bowing His head, He gave up His spirit."[29]

He even gave us a physical sign that the Old Covenant was over "Then, behold, the veil of the temple was torn in two from top to bottom; and the earth quaked, and the rocks were split." And since God always has to go the extra mile to get it through our thick heads and dull spirits in 70 AD the Romans fulfilled the prophecy of Jesus concerning

---

[28] Bible Gateway https://www.biblegateway.com/passage/?search=Matthew+22%3A37-40&version=NKJV 1-24-19
[29] Bible Gateway https://www.biblegateway.com/passage/?search=john+19%3A28-30&version=NKJV 1-24-19

Jerusalem and the Temple, "Do you not see all these things? Assuredly, I say to you, not one stone shall be left here upon another, that shall not be thrown down."[30]

No one not even the Jews can even attempt to fulfill the Law without the Temple and the sacrifices it calls for. So why are so many Christians trying to do it? Why are so many preachers and teachers leading people into a way that leads to a dead end?

Paul tried to warn us, "Christ has set us free to live a free life. So take your stand! Never again let anyone put a harness of slavery on you."[31]

And of course he had to explain this a little further so maybe we'd get the idea, "The moment any one of you submits to circumcision or any other rule-keeping system, at that same moment Christ's hard-won gift of freedom is squandered. I repeat my warning: The person who accepts the ways of circumcision trades all the advantages of the free life in Christ for the obligations of the slave life of the law."

And fearing even this was not enough he added, "When you attempt to live by your

---

[30] Bible Gateway https://www.biblegateway.com/passage/?search=Matthew+24%3A2&version=NKJV 1-24-19

[31] Bible Gateway https://www.biblegateway.com/passage/?search=galatians+5&version=MSG 1-24-19

own religious plans and projects, you are cut off from Christ, you fall out of grace. Meanwhile we expectantly wait for a satisfying relationship with the Spirit. For in Christ, neither our most conscientious religion nor disregard of religion amounts to anything. What matters is something far more interior: faith expressed in love."[32]

Isn't that plain. When we try to earn our way to heaven by keeping rules we're bound to fail because as soon as we accept anything as a "must do" the whole of the Law become a "better get it done." And no one can do it.

Paul laments that no matter how hard he tried it was impossible for him to keep all the law.[33] He realized this inability meant he was condemned no matter how good he tried to be. Because of that he cried, "O wretched man that I am! Who will deliver me from this body of death?"[34] And I believe anyone who is honest with themselves will admit we all have an apple out of that sack.

Luckily for us Paul also gave us the answer, "I thank God—through Jesus Christ our

---

[32] Bible Gateway https://www.biblegateway.com/passage/?search=galatians+5&version=MSG 1-24-19
[33] Bible Gateway https://www.biblegateway.com/passage/?search=romans+7&version=NKJV 1-24-19
[34] Bible Gateway https://www.biblegateway.com/passage/?search=romans+7%3A24&version=NKJV 1-24-19

Lord!"[35] for since we have been made alive in the Spirit towards God by being born-again we can also cry out with him, "So then, with the mind I myself serve the law of God, but with the flesh the law of sin."[36]

My advice: Die to the flesh and live to the Spirit. Discard the Old Law and embrace what Christ has done for us. He died to set us free so let's be free indeed.

---

[35] Bible Gateway
[36] Bible Gateway https://www.biblegateway.com/passage/?search=romans+7%3A25&version=NKJV 1-24-19

Reflection Six

Does God Speak to You?

Whenever people ask me this question, "Do you mean God speaks to you?" I answer it with another, "Do mean God doesn't speak to you?"

You can officially mark me down as a crazy person or whatever you like I don't care. But I initially turned from the world to face God because I heard a voice answer my silent plea, the plea of a lost and lonely sinner about to give up on life, "I've got to try something."

What I heard was a voice as real as any I've ever heard say right in my ear, "Why don't you try God."

As a militant atheist I turned to confront whoever it was that dared to say some invisible make-believe spirit might be the answer to my aching heart. There was no one there. At least there was no one there that I could see or find. So after an exhaustive search that turned up no one I started searching for who might have been there that I couldn't see. It was a search that eventually led me through the Gospels to Jesus. It was a search that led me from a dead-end life to a life filled with hope.

I said all that to say all this:

Have you ever felt God leading you to do something? It probably won't be an audible voice. I am convinced that God only uses an audible voice for either the extremely hard-hearted/hard-headed or to comfort the extremely hard pressed. Instead he leads us through our spirit which is linked to Him through His Spirit which lives in us as born-again believers.

If you aren't one of those it's easy just confess Jesus as Lord or leader of your life and believe in your heart that God raised Him from the dead...and that's it. Done and done.

So here we are children of God through adoption, made right with Him, spiritually standing in Daddy's throne room, minding our own business and His Spirit leads us to do something: something that doesn't seem like something we would want to do on your own.......say He leads us to spend everything we have to buy Bibles to give to homeless people.

What should we do?

I'm talking about spending way more money than our natural head says we can afford. It just doesn't make sense when we look at our budget through natural eyes. And the wisdom of the world tells us, "Come on most of the homeless you give a Bible will either lose it or throw it away." Or, "Come on they'll only listen to you witness about what Christ has done for you and accept the Bible so they can get a handout or something."

But there it is again, an urging, a leading to do this thing that makes no sense. It itches at our hearts. It won't leave. We feel our spirit saying, "If I don't do this I'll miss an opportunity to do what I'm supposed to do," while our head says, "Are you crazy you can't afford to do that!"

Over and over our heads, filled with natural sense knowledge keep shouting, "If I spend all that money just to give it away I won't have it for what I need." Or the ever ready, "Can't someone else do it? Like someone who has more money."

God isn't looking for ability He's looking for availability. If He can make donkeys speak and use murderers to being people back to life, turn water into wine, and save sinners like us He can surely provide for all our needs.

If we want to see the miracles of God we need to follow Him into uncharted water. We need to do what He calls us to do because where God guides God provides. Walking in faith always sensitive to what He calls us to do and then following Him in the doing … that's the way to see the miracles of God.

Faith isn't doing only what we can do on our own. Faith is doing what God calls us to do even when we know we can't. Let's step out of the boat and feel the waves beneath our feet.

Reflection Seven

Faith is the Answer and Prayer is the Key

It's time for us to grow up, to put away childish things and delve into the deep things of God.

Some may ask, "How do I do that?"

We need to study to show ourselves approved rightly dividing the word of God for it's sharper than a two edged sword or a surgeon's scalpel. It divides soul and spirit and it reveals all things. We need to speak to God and listen to God. We need to learn to hear His voice and recognize it. In other words we need to be in a constant conversation with God so that we can be about His business in this world.

Often we pray for God to guide our steps and then do nothing as we wait. God cannot guide our steps if we aren't stepping. Step out in faith and He'll sustain us as we work for Him. That's right. It may have been free admission but it isn't a free ride. God has called us to work. And He has given us the tool to do the work: faith.

Don't believe me believe Him.

It's impossible to please God apart from faith.[37] And why? Because anyone who wants to approach God must believe both that he exists *and* that he cares enough to respond to those who seek him. And part of that faith knows that He didn't send us out to work for Him without equipping us with what we need to accomplish that work.

Jesus said, "Believe me: I am in my Father and my Father is in me. If you can't believe that, believe what you see—these works. The person who trusts me will not only do what I'm doing but even greater things, because I, on my way to the Father, am giving you the same work to do that I've been doing. You can count on it. From now on, whatever you request along the lines of who I am and what I am doing, I'll do it. That's how the Father will be seen for who he is in the Son. I mean it. Whatever you request in this way, I'll do."[38]

And He didn't just say it once or twice. He said it over and over, "This is what I want you to do: Ask the Father for whatever is in keeping with the things I've revealed to you.

---

[37] Bible Gateway https://www.biblegateway.com/passage/?search=hebrews+11%3A6&version=MSG 1-24-19

[38] Bible Gateway https://www.biblegateway.com/passage/?search=john+14%3A13&version=MSG 1-24-19

Ask in my name, according to my will, and he'll most certainly give it to you."[39]

Jesus wasn't keeping this ability to accomplish the work He's called us to do miraculously through the power of His Name a secret. He told us numerous times that praying in His Name, in line with His purposes was more than just effective it's powerful.

He also told us that we've been chosen to do His work in the world in His Name, "You didn't choose me, remember; I chose you, and put you in the world to bear fruit, fruit that won't spoil. As fruit bearers, whatever you ask the Father in relation to me, he gives you."[40]

The time for hesitation is through. Once we confess Him as Lord and believe that God has raised Him from the dead we are born again. There's no time to linger at the edge of the pool waiting for someone else to do the heavy lifting. Dive head first into the deep end. Turn away from the weak and beggarly elements of this world and embrace life in His eternal presence which begins the moment we're born again and translated from the

---

[39] Bible Gateway https://www.biblegateway.com/passage/?search=john+16%3A23-24&version=MSG 1-24-19

[40] Bible Gateway https://www.biblegateway.com/passage/?search=john+15%3A16&version=MSG 1-24-19

kingdom of darkness in this world into the kingdom of light in His presence.

We all have questions for God. I know my first was "Why me." Then once we've taken up residence in His city on a hill we move on to, "What do You want me to do?" quickly followed by "How am I supposed to do that?" He isn't looking so much for ability as He is for availability. And remember: where God guides God provides. If He's called you to it you can do it. Just have faith, talk to Him, listen to Him, and watch as He turns your life into Acts Chapter twenty-nine.

Whatever questions, whatever problems, whatever opportunities we face in this life prayer is the answer and faith is the key.

Reflection Eight

Here's a Free Gift

As a retired pastor I am still amazed at the number of people who came forward week after week repenting of sins and seeking salvation. It was often the same people week after week. No matter how much I preached it, no matter how much I taught it, so many never seemed grasp the idea that the cleansing of sins, salvation, and righteousness are free gifts given to us by our Father.

People would cry, "I've been seeking after God for years. I've laid at the altar and pleaded over and over for God to guide me, to save me, to help me, and nothing happened. I leave the altar the same poor sinner as when I went up there."

My heart breaks for any and all who labor under such beggarly results.

My mind would scream as my voice would say, "Salvation is a gift. It isn't necessary for you to go anywhere to get it. You can find it anywhere. It isn't what you do, it's what Jesus has done. All there is to getting saved and to becoming a child of God is to receive something for free. You can't earn it by doing anything."

Most of us have been taught and have accepted that it was all about giving up, surrendering, and confessing sins. It isn't. It is receiving Jesus Christ as our Savior and confessing Him as our Lord.

I have had people say, "It can't be that simple."

It is that simple. It's free and it's available to everyone, everywhere, at all times.

Some have asked, "But don't we have to do something about our sins?"

No, He has done everything that ever could be done. And this isn't some new teaching or revelation. Our Father God told us about it through His prophet Isaiah long ago, "We're all like sheep who've wandered off and gotten lost. We've all done our own thing, gone our own way. And God has piled all our sins, everything we've done wrong, on him, on him."[41]

This is speaking about all of us. We have all gone our own way, done what we wanted without any reference to what God wanted us to do. We were stubborn and willful yet the Father laid the penalty for all that on Jesus. Notice there was nothing we had to do to save or help ourselves.

So how do we get from knowing this in our heads to having this become life in our hearts? John tells us, "as many as received

---

[41] Bible Gateway https://www.biblegateway.com/passage/?search=isaiah+53%3A6&version=MSG 1-25-19

Him, to them He gave the right to become children of God, to those who believe in His name."[42]

Once again we do nothing except receive a free gift.

John also tells us "For God so loved the world that He gave His only begotten Son, that whoever believes in Him should not perish but have everlasting life."[43] This is the Father giving His Son Jesus as our substitute, as our Savior and all He asks is that we accept Him for what He said He is. There is nothing for us to do except believe that He paid the debt owed for our sin and that He rose from the Dead to bring us life. Or as Paul put it, "who was delivered up because of our offenses, and was raised because of our justification."[44]

God delivered Jesus to pay the punishment for our sins and He was raised from the dead when He had paid the full measure, and all we have to do is accept that. We don't have to do anything to earn what He has already paid for.

Paul sums it all up well in the next verse when he says, "Therefore, having been

---

[42] Bible Gateway https://www.biblegateway.com/passage/?search=John+1%3A12&version=NKJV 1-25-19
[43] Bible Gateway https://www.biblegateway.com/passage/?search=john+3%3A16&version=NKJV 1-25-19
[44] Bible Gateway https://www.biblegateway.com/passage/?search=romans+4%3A25&version=NKJV 1-25-19

justified by faith, we have peace with God through our Lord Jesus Christ."[45]

Now besides salvation we have peace. There is nothing standing between us and God we are at peace and still there is nothing for us to do is there?

Paul tells us as clearly as can be how this all comes about and what the result is when he says, "that if you confess with your mouth the Lord Jesus and believe in your heart that God has raised Him from the dead, you will be saved. For with the heart one believes unto righteousness, and with the mouth confession is made unto salvation. For the Scripture says, "Whoever believes on Him will not be put to shame."

Look at that a little closer: when we confess with our mouth that Jesus is Lord that should be the end of us going our own way and doing our own thing. If you're anything like I was before I did this that shouldn't be too hard considering where our own choices and our own things have brought us. In other words if I relinquish being the Lord of my life and give that place to Jesus I will no longer be separated from God and I will become His child, a member of His family with all the rights and responsibilities that means.

If we do this what does the Word say? It says that we will be saved. When does it say we will be saved? It happens as soon as we

---

[45] Bible Gateway https://www.biblegateway.com/passage/?search=Romans+5%3A1&version=NKJV 1-25-19

believe. This isn't pie-in-the-sky. This is here and now reality. What does the Word say we are when we believe? It says we are now children of God. Does that mean now or someday way over there in the future when we get to heaven? No it says we have it now even if we don't know fully what that means. Or, as John put it, "now we are children of God; and it has not yet been revealed what we shall be, but we know that when He is revealed, we shall be like Him, for we shall see Him as He is."[46]

How do we know all this is true? How do we know that as soon as we confess and believe we are born again into a new life right here right now? John tells us, "These things I have written to you who believe in the name of the Son of God, that you may know that you have eternal life."

Having learned this do you believe in the Name of Jesus?

If you do then you have eternal life. Eternal life is the nature of God. That means you now have the nature of God. You are no longer a fallen sinner who needs to beg forgiveness you are filled with the very nature of God. Peter put it very clearly when he said, "by which have been given to us exceedingly great and precious promises, that through these you may be partakers of the divine nature, having escaped the corruption that is in the world through

---

[46] Bible Gateway https://www.biblegateway.com/passage/?search=I+john+3%3A2&version=NKJV 1-25-19

lust." That corruption is spiritual death and we have escaped it by receiving the divine nature: eternal life.

So don't fall into the trap of thinking you have to get good enough to get saved, or to see your life change. None of us could ever be that good. It isn't about what we do. It's about what He has done. It isn't about who we are. It's all about who He is. He paid the price. He purchased the freedom of all humans from the grip of Satan, and he extends that freely to all who believe He is who He said He is, that He rose from the dead and that He is the Savior of all who believe in Him.

Come on. It's free and it's yours for the taking. Why wait another moment. You can have it right here right now. Confess with your lips that Jesus is Lord and believe in your heart that God raised Him from the dead and it's yours.

Got it? Done it? Now tell someone. Shout it from the rooftops you are a child of God living an eternal life in fellowship with our Father. Welcome to the family.

Reflection Nine

How Can A Moral Wrong Be A Civil Right

As an American Historian my favorite area of study and discussion is the writing and ratification of the Constitution. It isn't because this is the beginning because the 167 year long colonial period became the world which birthed the Revolution, and without the Revolution there would be no America. So the colonial period is crucial for identifying many currents and trends in our society many of which still impact us today. Then why does this short period of one year capture my attention so much? Perhaps, it stands out because this is the cradle, the bedrock of American civil society. It is here that we can find the roots of the issue I wish to discuss today.

Labels are important.

The Revolution was fought not because of taxation. Remember the battle cry of the Revolutionaries was not the anarchist's "No Taxation!" It was instead the cry, "No taxation without representation!"[47] This was

[47] U.S. History https://www.u-s-history.com/pages/h640.html 1-25-19

not pulled from the heart of people who wanted to destroy the British Empire. It was not shouted from the lips of people who initially wanted to start a new country on the edge of wilderness thousands of miles from the center of everything they considered civilization. No it was the cry of people who sought for some level of local power. They wanted a voice and a vote in Parliament. What they wanted without vocalizing it was a federal system where there were defined levels of authority between a central government and a local one.

For most of the Colonial period the colonies had been allowed to run their local affairs. It is known as the period of Benign Neglect[48] when England more or less allowed the colonies to do as they wished, to establish local governments, and manage their own local affairs.

So after the massive expenses of the French and Indian War, which finally secured the American colonies from the fear of French attack, the British government sought to make the colonies help repay that debt through taxes. The fat hit the fire and Katie bar the door. This sparked the Revolution fought to secure the right to local

---

[48] British North America Power Point http://community.weber.edu/weberreads/salutary_or_benign_neglect.htm 1-25-19

government. The thirteen colonies all considered themselves independent States after the Declaration of Independence which expressly says:

That these united Colonies are, and of Right ought to be Free and Independent States, that they are Absolved from all Allegiance to the British Crown, and that all political connection between them and the State of Great Britain, is and ought to be totally dissolved; and that as Free and Independent States, they have full Power to levy War, conclude Peace, contract Alliances, establish Commerce, and to do all other Acts and Things which Independent States may of right do.

You can't be much clearer than that. Thirteen independent States formed a Confederation to fight the Revolution and to coordinate their foreign affairs. After the Revolution when this Confederation appeared too weak a central power for some it was brushed aside in what has been called a counter revolution. Remember the so-called Constitutional Convention[49] was called and empowered to merely draft suggested amendments to the Articles of Confederation. The Framers took it upon themselves to draft and entirely new government supplanting the one then in

---

[49] U.S. History https://www.u-s-history.com/pages/h368.html 1-25-19

existence. It was mainly the weight of Washington's name attached to the effort which gave it undefeatable currency among the people forcing the current government to agree to its own obsolescence.

Here is where the importance of labels manifests itself. The backers of the Constitution were in many cases wealthy and powerful men. They had powerful allies in the press. And in the ensuing debates that proponents of a strong central government were labeled the Federalists and those who opposed them were labeled the Anti-Federalists.

Besides the fact that "Anti" in front of anything certainly sounds and feels negative the reality is that the Federalists were the enemies of local authority. Hamilton, the leader of the Federalists in the debate, originally wanted a monarchy. And those opposing the Constitution wanted to keep the Confederation model of strong local authority and a loose central government. In other words, the opponents in this vital debate were intentionally mislabeled to confuse the voting public.

Fake news didn't begin with the Trump era and propaganda didn't begin with Hitler or Stalin.

If we look at the most famous artifacts of this debate the Federalist and Antifederalist

Papers we see that the Federalists led by Hamilton basically said whatever they had to in order to get the Constitution ratified. They magnified the weakness of the central government and exaggerated the authority of the States. Then as soon as the Constitution was ratified and they took over the new government Hamilton and his followers immediately began stretching the central power by re-interpreting such things as the Necessary and Proper Clause[50] and the Interstate Commerce Clause.[51] This continues to this day. Federalism which is the idea that there exists a separation between the sovereignty of the central government and the States continues to appear alive and well. There is a central government in Washington and State governments in all fifty States. However the Civil War radically changed the equation tipping the scales[52] forever in favor of the central government. The Supremacy Clause of thc Constitution reigns supreme as does the central government. Try to find somewhere in America today that is not regulated, monitored, or controlled by the ever growing tentacles of the Federal

---

[50] Freedom Works http://www.freedomworks.org/content/necessary-and-proper-clause-declaratory-truth 1-25-19

[51] The Heritage Foundation https://www.heritage.org/the-constitution/report/commerce-commerce-everywhere-the-uses-and-abuses-the-commerce-clause 1-25-19

[52] American Government http://www.ushistory.org/gov/3b.asp 1-25-19

Government. They're everywhere! They're everywhere!

I have said all that to say this.

Labels matter.

In a pivotal debate today the press is weighted heavily in favor of one side and solidly against another. They routinely portray one side positively and the other side as merely a negative of the side they are attempting to convince the public to support. What is this issue?

I believe abortion is a moral dilemma disguised as both a political debate and a religious issue. While it is certainly both I contend that at its heart lies a moral question whose answer will ultimately describe and define the reality of the three fundamental God-given rights for which the Revolution itself was fought to secure, "Life, Liberty, and the Pursuit of Happiness."[53]

There is no debate about the reality of what an abortion is and what it does. The science is all on one side. Life begins at conception.[54] A freshman in high school biology should be able to put that one and one makes two together.

---

[53] U.S.History.org http://www.ushistory.org/Declaration/document/ 1-25-19

[54] NAAPC https://naapc.org/why-life-begins-at-conception/ 1-25-19

Yet how is the public debate defined? How has it been defined for the many decades that it has occupied a prominent place on America's horizon?

Is it Pro-abortion and Pro-life? Two names which clearly describe the two positions. No it is defined as a debate between Pro-choice and Anti-abortion or Anti-choice, Pro-women's rights or Anti-women's rights.

Why did I start this article speaking about the Constitution? One, because it is a quintessential example of the power of labeling in a public debate, and two because looking at what this country was founded to secure brings us immediately to those God-given rights[55] we all love so much. The first of which is "Life."

We may call this a political debate between Republicans who are officially pro-life and Democrats who are officially pro-abortion. We may call it a religious debate between Christians, Muslims, and Jews who believe in the sacred sanctity of life and secularists who believe that one can be sacrificed for the convenience of another. We can be distracted by the carnival mirror reporting of the Corporations Once Called the Mainstream Media or we can

[55] U.S. History.org
http://www.ushistory.org/Declaration/document/ 1-25-19

look inside ourselves and let the voice of our conscious speak to the reality of our lives.

Murder by any other name is still murder. Murder is always and everywhere wrong. Does society need to do a better job educating people about the cause and effect of casual sex? Yes. Do we as Americans want a culture of life or a culture of death? The secularists demand that we look at the science when it comes to their Gia worship dressed up as man-made global warming so why don't we demand that they look at the science. Life begins at conception period. If reading studies or listening to lectures is too tedious to prove this fact, maybe looking at ultrasounds of pre-born in the womb sucking their thumb or scratching their head might help.

Now back to the Constitution.

Those who seek to advance the Living Constitution model basically say that what the Framers believed was carved in stone was actually written in sand. Through their interminable twists and turns of literary interpretation legerdemain they seem unable to understand that the Second Amendment actually means what the words say. However, they have been miraculously able to stretch the Fourth Amendment to confer a right to privacy which is then stretched to say the right to an abortion, which was considered an abomination during the time of the Framers, was somehow implied in there some place.

The Constitution which was written to establish and maintain a limited government is now elastic enough to empower the leviathan along the Potomac. And the Revolution which was meant to secure our God-given right to Life, Liberty, and the Pursuit of Happiness has morphed into the ultimate evil state approved and funded murder.

This all leaves me with a final question. How can a moral wrong be a civil right?

Reflection Ten

Hunker in the Bunker and Wait for the Rain

As those of you who follow these wandering pages know I have recently re-aligned my life to turn and face the strange changes[56] that are overtaking Western Civilization with ever increasing speed. Like ripples whose shape and size shifts but never leave the stream, change is the only constant in a society careening towards a cliff.

The descendants of those who built the empire no longer produce enough children to man the walls. The will to win and the desire to excel has been replaced by a complacency bred of bread, circuses, and entitlement checks distributed by a perpetually re-elected legislature designed to keep the marks from catching the con. A series of lack-luster presidents set the stage for collapse. One declares a new world order and then loses his bid for re-election to a saxophone playing party-boy. This surprise president sets the morality bar so low his scurrilous actions and obvious lack of character corrupt the very

[56] David Bowie http://www.guntheranderson.com/v/data/changes.htm 1-25-19

fiber of our nation. The next two expand the government and spend us into oblivion.

Empires rise and empires fall. That is the way of the world and the lesson of History. From the 15th century through the 20th Western Civilization used a temporary advantage in technology to conquer the world. Where our military conquered we imposed our culture. Where we didn't gain political control the vision of our seemingly invulnerable strength and our unstoppable progress led local leaders to discard much of what was theirs to imitate what they coveted of ours.

For five centuries Western Civilization ruled supreme. It was our way or the highway so in our pride we decided ours was the High Way. Then in two spectacular bouts of societal suicide, World War I and World War II, we killed, maimed, and butchered ourselves. We wasted the accumulated riches of centuries and showed the millions of colonial subject people who were brought in to help kill whoever the enemy happened to be that Westerners weren't invulnerable, weren't unconquerable, and weren't even smart enough to avoid the slaughter or hide the evidence.

The destruction of the economies and populations of the various colonial powers inevitably led to the break-up of the empires and the rise of a bi-polar world that pitted a world-wide Communism that was inimical to everything Western Civilization stood for against a united West now led by the newest edition to their ranks: the United States.

We had allied ourselves with the Communists to defeat the Fascists. However the victory of 1945 vanished into fifty years of a Cold War that flashed hot enough times to kill many tens of thousands. This epic struggle brought the Communists to their knees and us to the edge of bankruptcy. As we defeated Communism its less threatening little brother Socialism crept in the back door. We adopted the tenants of socialism: equality of outcome financed by expropriation and wealth and re-distribution to pacify our population through the long war. Today we are fast becoming all we have fought against for the last sixty years: a centrally-planned economy, a regimented society, and a totalitarian state.

This century long series of debilitating wars sapped our will to reproduce just as technology gave us birth control and lax morals gave us abortion. This unholy trinity turned into a demographic time bomb that ensures the eventual submerging of the peoples of the West beneath waves of immigrants swarming in to take their place. The moral rot swilled out from Hollywood, and a reality show culture exemplified and condoned by the political elite inspires and reflects a hedonism that would have made Caligula blush. The entitlement mentality foisted and fostered by buy-a-vote-with-benefits governments has sapped people of the drive and desire to do anything more than sit on a couch and dream of their chance at the golden ring of fifteen minutes of fame.

Sounds like a dismal picture doesn't it? The most depressing part of the whole thing is that it is true.

Empires rise and empires fall and it is our lot to live on the declining end of Western Civilization: the greatest empire of all time (so far).

No one ever gets to live in the world they were raised in. Time moves on and things change. However most generations don't watch the inversion of the world they grew up in. Today things we thought were wrong are now right. Things we thought werc right are now wrong. What made you healthy yesterday kills you today. The wisdom of the ancients was once sought after in a world of constants today obsolesce often proceeds production in a microwave throw-away culture.

The world has been turned upside down.

Just as a British general marched out of Yorktown to surrender to a rag-tag bunch of summer soldiers, so we the children of those who stormed the beaches on D-Day to free Europe and end the darkness that was Nazism will wonder how were we defeated by those we had once so easily dominated?

The answer will be the same as it was for the British in the Revolution and for the Nazis in World War II: we defeated ourselves. Our over confidence and our desire to have it all led us to forsake the values that brought about our success and the principles that made us who we were. While the Socialist Progressives march us off to the shabby future they have centrally-planned perhaps instead of the World Turned Upside Down we should sing a paraphrase of a line from the sixties, "In tattered tuxedos they face the new heroes and crawl about in confusion. All the hands raised; they stand there amazed at the shattering of their illusions."[57]

We stand at the edge of the abyss. We know not what will be only that it will not be what it has been. Do not despair. Do not lose hope. Have faith in Christ. Follow Him and He will guide you to a safe harbor amidst the storm. I have found my place. I am preparing every day for the coming

[57] Cowboy Lyrics .com https://cowboylyrics.com/lyrics/ochs-phil/ringing-of-revolution-11450.html#.T89_a8X-5p8 1-25-19

crescendo. My best advice is find Christ, find your place, and hunker down.

Keep the faith. Keep the peace. We shall overcome.

Reflection Eleven

I Got Faith You Got Faith All God's Children Got Faith

Pastor John Osteen the father of Mega Church Joel used to lead his congregation in this confession, "This is my Bible. I am what it says I am. I have what it says I have. I can do what it says I can do." while waving his big black Bible in the air. He started every service this way encouraging the faithful to stand on God's Word.

It's our confession of God's Word that opens the door to miracles. For if we don't believe God's Word how can we say we believe God? And if we don't believe God who and what do we believe?

Many of us have been told we're losers. Many of us have been told we're worthless, unwanted, unnecessary, and unloved. Not all of us grew up with Mom and Pop Cleaver protecting, supporting, and affirming us. Many of us have told ourselves we're no good, forgotten, and useless. And sad to say many of us believe what the world says about us. We often believe ourselves and allow these beliefs to shape and guide our lives.

May be we should try God? Let's believe His Word and let that shape and guide our lives.

Now think about God's Word for a moment. He says[58] that His word[59] is truth,[60] and that His judgments endure forever. He also says He watches over His Word to perform it.[61] If He's lying about all that He's a liar, and we know God isn't a liar. The devil is.[62] That's his very nature. And since the devil's original sin[63] was his desire to be recognized as God, when we say or act as if God is a liar we're giving the devil exactly what he wants, because we're saying the liar is our God.

---

[58] Bible Gateway https://www.biblegateway.com/passage/?search=Psalm+119%3A160&version=NKJV 1-25-19
[59] Bible Gateway https://www.biblegateway.com/passage/?search=2+Samuel+7%3A28&version=NKJV 1-25-19
[60] Bible Gateway https://www.biblegateway.com/passage/?search=John+17%3A17&version=NKJV 1-25-19
[61] Bible Gateway https://www.biblegateway.com/passage/?search=Jeremiah+1%3A12&version=NKJV 1-25-19
[62] Bible Gateway https://www.biblegateway.com/passage/?search=John+8%3A44&version=NKJV 1-25-19
[63] Bible Gateway https://www.biblegateway.com/passage/?search=Isaiah+14%3A13&version=NKJV 1-25-19

Spiritual things can only be understood[64] by those who are spiritual. To the natural man they're foolishness[65] and the fool has said[66] in his heart there is no God. In this article I'm speaking to believers and hopefully to those without hope who might become believers. To those who've confessed Jesus as Lord and who believe in their heart that God raised Him from the dead. If we've done those things His Word says we will be saved.[67] It doesn't say might be. It doesn't say could be. It says will be. Which also means you can be.

He also says we overcame the devil by the blood of the Lamb AND the word of our testimony,[68] that we will be judged by the words[69] that come out of our mouth, and that whatever we ask in the name of Jesus[70] we shall receive that the Father may be glorified in the Son.

---

[64] Bible Gateway https://www.biblegateway.com/passage/?search=1+Corinthians+2%3A13-15&version=NKJV 1-25-19

[65] Bible Gateway https://www.biblegateway.com/passage/?search=1+Corinthians+2%3A13-15&version=NKJV 1-25-19

[66] Bible Gateway https://www.biblegateway.com/passage/?search=psalm+14%3A1&version=NKJV 1-25-19

[67] Bible Gateway https://www.biblegateway.com/passage/?search=romans+10%3A9&version=NKJV 1-25-19

[68] Bible Gateway https://www.biblegateway.com/passage/?search=REV+12%3A11&version=NKJV 1-25-19

[69] Bible Gateway https://www.biblegateway.com/passage/?search=Matthew+12%3A37+&version=NKJV 1-25-19

[70] Bible Gateway

That is some powerful stuff. Our words are important. Some people interpret all this in such a way that believe God becomes their servant and that He's honor bound to give us anything we ask for. But in His Word He tells us that we need to ask for the right stuff when He says you ask and don't receive,[71] because you ask amiss, that you may spend it on your pleasures.

We need to get lined up with Him. We need to allow Him to put the desires in our heart[72] and then use the power of confession in the Name of Jesus to move forward in the ministry He's called us to, and then we'll receive the desires of our heart, the ones He put there. For make no mistake if you're a believer you've been called to minister the Word to a world dying to receive it. That ministry is your witness.[73] You don't have to be a Bible scholar. God will always give you the words to say if you testify of Him.[74] Share your witness, your testimony. Simply tell what the Lord has

---

[71] Bible Gateway https://www.biblegateway.com/passage/?search=+James+4%3A3&version=NKJV 1-25-19

[72] Bible Gateway https://www.biblegateway.com/passage/?search=psalm+37%3A4&version=NKJV 1-25-19

[73] Bible Gateway https://www.biblegateway.com/passage/?search=acts+1%3A8&version=NKJV 1-25-19

[74] Bible Gateway https://www.biblegateway.com/passage/?search=luke+12%3A12&version=NKJV 1-25-19

done for you. And if you don't have a testimony, seek the Lord until you have one.

All it takes is faith to walk out on God's Word and expect Him to accomplish it. That's what we do to get saved. And that's what we must do to be who He says we are, to have what He says we have, and to do what He's called us to do.

And if the believers among us think we don't have enough faith remember we had enough faith to believe God for salvation. And I don't know about you but if I have enough faith to believe God will welcome someone like me into heaven I've got more than a mustard seed's worth so mountain you better start jumping.[75] Also remember faith itself is a gift from God.[76] We can always ask for more.[77] So if you don't have enough faith to believe God for salvation, ask God and He will give it to you.

I got faith, you got faith, all God's children got faith, and the only kind of faith for me is faith in Jesus Christ.

---

[75] Bible Gateway https://www.biblegateway.com/passage/?search=matthew+17%3A20&version=NKJV 1-25-19
[76] Bible Gateway https://www.biblegateway.com/passage/?search=Ephesians+2%3A8&version=NKJV 1-25-19
[77] Bible Gateway https://www.biblegateway.com/passage/?search=Mark+9%3A24-25&version=NKJV 1-25-19

Reflection Twelve

I'm Blessed

When asked by the Barna Group, "Do we have a personal responsibility to share our faith with others?"[78] a majority of Christians answer in the affirmative.

100% of Evangelicals and 73% of born again Christians said yes. When this conviction is put into practice however, the numbers shift downward. Only 69% of Evangelicals and 52% of born again Christians say they actually did share the Gospel at least once this past year to someone with different beliefs in the hope that they might accept Jesus Christ as their Savior.

"Born again Christians" were defined in these surveys as people who said they have made "a personal commitment to Jesus Christ that is still important in their life today" and who also indicated they believe that when they die they will go to Heaven because they had confessed their sins and had accepted Jesus Christ as their savior. Respondents were not asked to describe themselves as "born

[78] Barna https://www.barna.com/research/is-evangelism-going-out-of-style/ 1-25-19

again." Being classified as "born again" is not dependent upon church or denominational affiliation or involvement.

"Evangelicals" meet the born again criteria described above plus seven other conditions. Those include: saying their faith is very important in their life today; believing they have a personal responsibility to share their religious beliefs about Christ with non-Christians; believing that Satan exists; believing that eternal salvation is possible only through grace, not works; believing that Jesus Christ lived a sinless life on earth; asserting that the Bible is accurate in all the principles it teaches; and describing God as the all-knowing, all-powerful, perfect deity who created the universe and still rules it today. Being classified as an evangelical is not dependent upon church attendance, the denominational affiliation of the church attended, or self-identification.

Many people have a hard time sharing their faith in Christ. They feel as if they don't want to be perceived as pushy. Possibly they're afraid to speak to strangers or they don't know how to get a conversation to a place where speaking about faith might be appropriate.

Here's an easy, comfortable way that my wife introduced me to many years ago.

In America a common greeting is, "Hi how're you doing?"

Most people aren't really concerned with how we're doing it's just a greeting. However, when someone asks us a question we're free to answer it and it's a natural and comfortable thing to do.

Whenever I'm asked America's greeting "Hi how're you doing?"

I answer, "I'm blessed."

The reactions are very interesting. Some just give a quizzical look. Some say, "You are?" which is another question.

And as in the initial situation answering a question is an easy natural thing to do. I'll answer, "You are?" with something like "I am and I won't accept anything less."

Sometimes people will answer with another question something like, "Why are you blessed?" and this opens the door for easily speaking about Jesus gave it to me and the world can't take it away or some other friendly answer that leads directly to speaking of Jesus. Not often but every once in a while it leads to an actual chance to share the hope of the Gospel. If nothing else it opens the door to speak the name of Jesus in public. And you never know who might be listening and what the sound of that Name may have in the ripple effect of reality.

Sometimes our initial response of "I'm blessed" is met with, "I am too." This opens a door for fellowship with a fellow believer and the collateral opportunity for others to hear people who aren't afraid to share their faith in public and another opportunity to speak the Name of Jesus into the air of a world that needs him.

This type of conversational evangelism is reflected in one T-shirt I have. It says, "I'm Blessed" and then under that large headline it offers an answer to anyone who might ask why, "You better ask Jesus."

It's also reflected in the words to an old song from the hills of Missouri:

I'm Blessed and I know that I am since Jesus took control of my life.

I'm blessed and I know that I am since He gave to me a new life.

I'm blessed and if you happen to ask how I am my friend.

I'm Blessed, I'm Blessed, I'm Blessed

So for any of us who find it hard to get started with sharing the good news of the Gospel with others why not give, "I'm blessed," a try since we are. Then get ready to walk through any doors God decides to open.

Reflection Thirteen

Is America Under Judgment?

All that follows I will preface with, "I believe." I am not attempting to establish theology for anyone or to declare that anyone who does not agree with me is a heretic. I am merely sharing my beliefs, grounded on study and prayer, since my opinion has been solicited on this topic more than once.

Many Christians today bring every conversation back to, "Do you think these are the last days?"

This may be based on a personal reading of the Book of Revelation in the Bible. It could be based on the broadcast sermons and teachings of any number of professional End Times preachers who have built careers on pointing to an apocalypse around the corner.

The signs of the times are always easy to read they just aren't so easy to interpret. Nero was the Antichrist as was Diocletian, King James II, Napoleon, Hitler, Stalin, and Mao. False Prophets have equally abounded from the Pope to Martin Luther, from Henry VIII to Rasputin to Jim Jones.

Is the End coming? Most certainly. Can we know when it is coming? Most certainly not. Since it is impossible to know when the end is coming I cannot believe that God would want us wasting any of the precious time He gives us speculating as to when it will arrive instead of being His witnesses to the world.

Since it is anti-biblical to believe we can know the date of the End, it is obviously not a Godly use of our time to try and figure it out anyway. What can we know? Just as we can look at the clouds and know when a storm is coming or smell the wind and know when a rain is on the way, so to we can look at the present state of our nation and know the time of the season. If we use the analogy of a year's cycle it is obviously fall headed for the winter. It has been fall headed for the winter since the crucifixion of Christ: the fulcrum of History.

Some may ask, "Why has fall lasted so long?" The problem is we really don't know how long the previous winter and spring were. The belief that the Bible tells us that there were approximately X number of thousand years before Christ and there will be X number of years after Christ equaling 7,000 years as a week in God's time as taught by some popular TV preachers is based on the a tissue of strung together scriptures and cherry-picked verses. Equally, the belief that the time from Adam and Christ is discernible from the Biblical text is based on the erroneous belief that the Bible is presented as a linear historical document.

While I believe that the Bible contains real History and that it is literally true I do not believe that it presents a year for year time-line type of presentation. The Old Testament is above all a spiritual History of how God chose one people and eventually one person to bring forth the Chosen One: Jesus Christ, the Messiah of the Jews and the Savior of man. I do not believe that by counting up the lives of everyone mentioned in Old Testament genealogies it is possible to know how many years elapsed between "Let there be light" and the birth, death, or resurrection of Christ.

Most of the names mentioned in the many Old Testament genealogies have no age associated with them so the would-be Biblical time liner has to make a guess. Also when you compare the genealogies there are obvious overlaps, repetitions, and omissions. Compare the New Testament genealogies of Christ found in Luke and in Matthew and you will see the problem with genealogies as linear History.[79] Now multiply that by all the genealogies in the Old Testament and you will begin to see the problem with this method of calculating time.

---

[79] ThoughtCo https://www.thoughtco.com/genealogy-of-jesus-700161 1-25-19

The people who tell us that the Old Testament gives us an accurate count of the years between the beginning and the beginning of the end are the same ones who tell us that they can figure out from the book of Revelation when the end of time will come. They do this in spite of the fact that Christ Himself tells us in Matthew, "But about that day or hour no one knows, not even the angels in heaven, nor the Son, but only the Father."[80] Then to make the point again it was one of the last things He told us before ascending to Heaven in Acts, "It is not for you to know times or seasons which the Father has put in His own authority."[81]

Since we cannot know the day or the hour, the times or the seasons how godly can it be to spend so much time trying to figure it out? So much for trying to figure out when THE end is since it can't be done. However, I felt I had to deal with that before I moved on to the real subject of this column: whether or not America is under judgment.

I believe that is a topic that can be discerned by anyone with eyes to see and ears to hear. I am not talking about the end of the United States. It is and will be called by the same

---

[80] Bible Hub https://biblehub.com/niv/matthew/24-36.htm 1-25-19

[81] Bible Gateway https://www.biblegateway.com/passage/?search=acts%201:7&version=NKJV 1-25-19

name, waving the same flag. I will let you judge if it is the same country we grew up in.

Looking at the spiritual History of the Old Testament as a guide we see that Judah the southern kingdom of the Jews, the believing remnant that carried on the covenant after the apostatized Kingdom of Israel had been carried off into exile was finally delivered into the hands of its enemies because they had sacrificed their children to pagan gods and walked in the ways of the world.[82] Since 1972 when a case based on a lie was used by an activist Supreme Court[83] to invent a constitutional right to abort babies over 60 million Americans have been deprived of the most fundamental right of all: Life.[84]

God does not condemn societies because of the sin within them because the same sins are in all peoples at all times. Rather God condemns societies for the sins they condone. Sodom, Gomorrah, and the cities of the plains were not destroyed because they were filled with more evil than the Canaanites that God eventually sent the Israelites to destroy. No, these cities were consumed by fire and brimstone because they gloried in what others did in shame.

---

[82] Bible Gateway https://www.biblegateway.com/passage/?search=2%20Kings%2021:5-13&version=NKJV 1-25-19
[83] @4 Years http://www.pregnantpause.org/abort/lies.htm 1-25-19
[84] Life News https://www.lifenews.com/2018/01/18/60069971-abortions-in-america-since-roe-v-wade-in-1973/ 1-25-19

Stroll down the streets of San Francisco. Flip the dial from the Modern Family to Two and a Half Men from The Jersey Shore to Glee and it seems Jerry Springer has defined the new America. On cable and satellite hard core porn fills the overnight hours while state after state legalizes pot on their way to legalizing everything. The government has taken over the numbers racket, calling it a lottery as they plunder the poorest amongst us by selling them false hope where winning is as likely as being struck with lightening.

What is the judgment of God on nations that have moved out from under His blessing by rejecting His guidance? He casts them down from the heights their former obedience had achieved. In the near future we may become the tail instead of the head as our leaders continue to wag the dog.

Alexis de Tocqueville one of the most astute observers of America said in the early 1800's "America is great because she is good, and if America ever ceases to be good, America will cease to be great." Now survey the current state of America for yourself. Don't accept the opinion of someone else, but make up your own mind.

Is America good? The answer to that will provide the answer to the question posed in the title of this column "Is America under

Judgment?" For if we are not good what are we? And what is the result of that?

If you decide for yourself that America is under judgment does that mean you should run for the nearest exit or hide in a fallout shelter?

Remember God has told those who follow Him, "A thousand may fall at your side, and ten thousand at your right hand; but it shall not come near you."[85]

Don't hide run. Run to the nearest rooftop and proclaim Jesus as Lord. Share your witness everywhere with everyone you can for it will only be through a renewal of the heart that we will come to the heart of the problem.

Keep the Faith. Keep the peace. We shall overcome.

---

[85] Bible Gateway https://www.biblegateway.com/passage/?search=Psalm%2091:7&version=NKJV 1-25-19

Reflection Fourteen

Jump!

Christ came to fulfill the Old Covenant. He paid the price for Adam's sin and made a way back into fellowship with God. Sin was the problem and Jesus is the answer.

When he was offered up by the High Priest as a sinless sacrifice He fulfilled all that had ever been required in the Old Covenant.

When He breathed His last on the cross and cried out, "It is finished," the curtain in the temple was ripped in half. God left the Holy of Holies on earth signifying the end of the Old Covenant. When Christ rose from the dead and ascended into heaven He poured out his blood on the eternal alter of God in the heavenly temple of God. All the sacrifices of the Old Testament had been but a foreshadowing of this event.

When we confess Jesus as Lord and believe in our heart that God raised Him from the dead as it says in Romans 10:9-10 we shall be saved.[86] It doesn't say we might be

---

[86] Bible Gateway https://www.biblegateway.com/passage/?search=romans+10%3A9-10&version=NKJV 1-25-19

saved. It doesn't say we will be saved by and by. It says we shall be saved. The moment we do that we're born again, recreated, and translated from the old world of sin caused separation from God and death to the new world of fellowship with God and life.

Once we're saved from the curse of sin we become the righteousness of God. This means we can stand in the presence of God without any guilt, shame, or fear for we've become His children. And as His children we have the right and the ability to come boldly into our Daddy's throne room any time we want.

Think of it this way, if you or I walked up to the gate of Buckingham Palace and told the guard, "Let me in I want to see the queen" we wouldn't even get a smile from one of those guys. But if Prince Phillip walked up and said the same thing they would immediately usher him into the royal presence.

It's the same with us and the heavenly Holy of Holies. God is our Father. We can enter His presence any time we want. There's no need to beg or plead. It's our right as His child because we are one with Christ. He's the head and we're the body. We're the very living stones built up into His eternal temple.

We're individually the tabernacles of His Holy Spirit who dwells in us.

Don't accept less. Be all that God re-created you to be. We're a new creation the old has passed away and behold all has become new. We dwell this moment in God's New Jerusalem and collectively we are His Holy Temple. God the Father is on His throne. Christ the Lamb that was slain for the sins of the world and yet lives is seated to His right hand. The Holy Spirit indwells the temple built of living stones.

There is nothing left to be done. It is finished. There is nothing we can add. We have been given the authority to act in the Name of Christ. We shouldn't sit back waiting to get good enough. We shouldn't expect some hireling to do what God has called us to do. We've been called to take the light of Christ into a world of darkness.

He never told us to build a lamp. He never told us to pay a lighthouse tender. He told us to take the light of His love to those sold under bondage to the king of this world. And we must always remember greater is He who is in us than he who is in the world.

Jesus told us that if we have faith, even if it's as small as the smallest seed, and we tell the mountain to jump it'll jump. So let's quit waiting for some collective bulldozer to move the mountains and start living as what we are: children of the Most High God.

In the desert God told Moses to speak to the rock. He has told us to speak to the mountains. So now, all together on the count of three let's say to the mountains in our life, "Jump!" One, Two, Three.

Reflection Fifteen

The god Particle I Don't Think So

Arrogance is a funny thing. Not Ha Ha funny, but funny none-the-less. I was watching one of America's leading physicists the other day, a man made famous by his co-authorship of String Theory and made popular by his ability to make people without a scientific education believe they understand what he's talking about.[87] He repeatedly made the statement that today physicists understand 99.9%of how the Universe works and that the .01% that was missing is the never before seen but previously postulated Higgs Boson particle[88] popularly known as the god particle.[89]

The reason he was on a popular news show was because other scientists in Switzerland had announced that they had found the ever elusive god particle by producing a mini-Big Bang in the world's largest cyclotron by smashing atoms together.[90] The Big Bang is

---

[87] Michio Kaku http://mkaku.org/ 1-25-19
[88] Fox News https://www.foxnews.com/science/the-elusive-particle-5-implications-of-finding-higgs-boson 1-25-19
[89] ABC News https://abcnews.go.com/Technology/higgs-boson-evidence-god-particle-reported-fermilab-physicists/story?id=16695742#.UDP0O6NbL2I 1-25-19
[90] USA Today https://usatoday30.usatoday.com/tech/science/space/story/20

what atheist scientists have to call creation because all their evidence proves that the universe, just started. They have come to believe that at one moment there was nothing and then a split nano-second later there was everything. Since they find it impossible to believe that God merely said, "Let there be" and it was they instead have mentally manufactured the Big Bang Theory, which along with the Theory of Evolution is taught to every school child as if it were established fact.

The Big Bang Theory goes like this: once upon a time there was nothing except the tiniest of points that contained the essence of everything. They even say there was no time because time itself was nonexistent before the Big Bang. Then spontaneously this tiniest of points exploded and in a flash it expanded into gases and stars and planets and galaxies. Using rooms full of chalk boards these highly educated scientists prove that all of everything came from something: a teeny tiny point of compressed something.

They piously tell us all their observations prove this is so. All their chalk filled blackboards prove this is so. All their experiments prove this is so. And now after they have discovered 99.9% of the truth the production of the missing god particle

---

12-07-05/Higgs-boson-explanation-particle-physics/56045722/1 1-25-19

absolutely proves it is so.[91] Just give them a little more time and they will be able to tell us exactly how the universe created itself.

How nice.

Luckily there are these eloquent popularizers who are able to act as a verbal interface allowing the scientifically and mathematically challenged masses peek behind the curtain. It's a good thing because it is our tax money that pays for all their orbiting telescopes, cyclotrons, and blackboards. And since the majority of us are Christians who believe God created the world it's convenient to have someone to explain to us why all the money we spend proves we are actually deluded provincials with a quaint faith in an unseen Father who created and upholds everything with His word, wrote a book to tell us about it, and then sent His only Son to die at our hands for our redemption.

Now that is money well spent. Pay billions and billions to have scientific shamans to tell us that what we believe are fables and what they believe is fact. Maybe we should spend our billions on magic beans instead, and then we could climb up to heaven and find out what really happened. Or maybe we should build a tower that reaches into heaven so our priest-king-scientist could give God a

---

[91] Health News https://www.moneylife.in/article/the-god-particle-unscientific-claims/27870.html 1-25-19

physical, and then tell us all about why He isn't there.

Our super smart highly educated and well financed scientists tell us they don't operate on faith; instead they operate on logic and objective evidence. Yet when you examine their chain of thought and peer into their evidence it is a fabric of conjectures based upon one leap of faith after another. They have convinced themselves the air castles they have constructed are more than science fiction, but why should we believe them? They do sound sincere and they do act as if they know what they are talking about, but so does the flim-flam man who tries to sell us the Brooklyn Bridge or the politician who tells us they can manage the debt and give everyone everything.

For one thing their very confidence that they have the universe 100% or even 99.9% figured out ought to tell us these wizards aren't ever going to really give us a heart, or courage, and certainly not a brain. They may give us a medal or a degree and then explain how they are just what they promised when they aren't but they can't deliver on the real thing. When Toto finally pulls the curtain back will we then realize we have spent billions upon billions to supposedly prove fantasies labeled as truth when we have had the truth all along: God created the universe, and we are here because of Him, in Him, and for Him. That may be too simplistic for the wizards to believe but their flights of fancy ought to be too fantastic for us to swallow.

For instance all these grand theories of everything never tell us where the incredibly compressed point comes from. They never tell us how long the point was in a state of perfect equilibrium just hanging there in the nothing. They never tell us what would have caused the point to explode. Yet they try to tell us they have it all figured out. Go figure.

I find it comical that believing in an all-knowing all-powerful God who created everything and everyone is too hard for people to believe but when a highly educated, highly financed, and media savvy spokes model tells us that everything created itself millions of people nod their heads and stand in line to give them more money for more experiments and blackboards so that we can expand our knowledge to what 110%?

This all reminds me of two things.

One:

There have been other times when societies and their wizards thought they knew everything.

A man named Ptolemy once proved that the whole universe revolves around the earth.[92] Eventually a complicated model was constructed by dedicated mathematicians and philosophers to demonstrate and prove how it worked.[93] Galileo among others was arrested, tried, and convicted for saying the Earth revolves around the Sun.[94] Once the alchemists knew there was a philosopher's stone that would turn iron into gold.[95] At one point the leading lights of science knew the world was flat while Columbus knew he could sail from Europe to Asia in a straight line. In the 1890s scientists assured us we knew everything about everything. Now the Big Bang explains it all and the god particle is the key to understanding how nothing became everything.

Two:

All these theories of everything that eliminate God remind me of the story about a scientist who when asked where his computer came from didn't know so he said, "There was a pile of parts laying in a junk yard for billions of years and one day they were struck by

---

[92] Claudius Ptolomy http://www-history.mcs.st-and.ac.uk/Biographies/Ptolemy.html 1-25-19
[93] M. S. Mahoney http://www.princeton.edu/~hos/mike/texts/ptolemy/ptolemy.html 1-25-19
[94] Galileo https://starchild.gsfc.nasa.gov/docs/StarChild/whos_who_level2/galileo.html 1-25-19
[95] Encyclopedia Britannica https://www.britannica.com/topic/philosophers-stone 1-25-19

lightning and out popped this computer." This scientist had a blackboard full of equations that proved he was right. He had spent billions of tax dollars conducting of experiments that proved he was right. And he sounded very convincing when he explained it all. His theory was accepted and taught in all the schools, so now our children can come home and tell us where computers come from.

And the cow jumped over the moon.

It also reminds me of the story about a scientist who said to God, "You're not so much. I've figured out how to create life in my laboratory."

"You have?" said God.

"Yes I have and I'm willing to have a competition to prove I can create life just like you," said the scientist as he wrote two rooms full of equations to show God how much he knew.

"Okay," said God as He stooped down picked up some dirt and started fashioning a man.

The scientist picked up some dirt and started pouring it from one test tube to another when God smiled and said, "Hey! Get your own dirt."

Even if we can prove how something happened does that tell us why? Since every chain of events has to have a beginning our wizards have had to come face-to-face with "In the beginning." However, without faith they can't see the forest for the tree. So instead of giving God the glory for his creation they try to construct creation without a creator, which reminds me of the atheist who knows there is no heaven and prays there is no hell.

I love to listen to the wizards. I read their books and watch their shows. However, I march to the beat of a different drummer, "And if it seems evil to you to serve the Lord, choose for yourselves this day whom you will serve, whether the gods which your fathers served that *were* on the other side of the River, or the gods of the Amorites, in whose land you dwell. But as for me and my house, we will serve the Lord."

Reflection Sixteen

The Heart of the Problem is in the Heart

Benjamin Franklin told us, "Only a virtuous people are capable of freedom. As nations become corrupt and vicious, they have more need of masters."[96]

Socialism is a debilitating confidence game dressed up as an ideology used by demagogues and want-to-be dictators to fool its victims into believing it is possible to have your cake and eat it too. Those who fall under the spell of the charlatans singing this siren song actually come to believe it is fair and just to force some people to labor for the good of others. This is the same type of sophistry and rationalization that was used by the clergy and philosophers of the Antebellum South to justify unending human bondage for an entire race of people because it was for their own good.

This twisted tool of central planners and bureaucratic tyrants teaches those who have not that it is fair and just to take from those

---

[96] Good Reads https://www.goodreads.com/quotes/438662-only-a-virtuous-people-are-capable-of-freedom-as-nations 1-26-19

who have and re-distribute the plunder as the government decrees. This is not fair! This is not just! To teach that it is raises up generations of people who believe they have a birth-right to that which is not their own forfeiting their true birth-right: the opportunity to succeed through their own efforts. The products of such an educational system are citizens without virtue voting pawns without honor. Not because they have made a personal decision to live without these two attributes but because they have been programmed to believe taking the fruit of someone else's labor is permissible as long as it will be given to someone else. Theodore Roosevelt said, "To educate a man in mind and not in morals is to educate a menace to society."[97]

Those who drank the Kool-Aid dispensed by the government schools learned that this type of theft is not only permissible it is laudable. They were told and they believe that this is what Robin Hood did: steal from the rich to give to the poor. However, in reality the legend of Robin Hood tells of a fighter for liberty and the sanctity of personal property who robbed the stolen wealth of corrupt government officials so that he could return it to its rightful owners: those who produced the wealth in the first place.

[97] Quotes on Liberty and Virtue http://www.liberty1.org/virtue.htm 1-26-19

However, the leaders of those wishing to turn America into a Venezuelan style worker's paradise have turned the world upside down demanding that people objectified by the name "Millionaires and Billionaires"[98] need to pay their fair share. Yet they never say what that fair share is or when enough will ever be enough. According to Noah Webster, "...if the citizens neglect their Duty and place unprincipled men in office, the government will soon be corrupted; laws will be made, not for the public good so much as for selfish or local purposes; corrupt or incompetent men will be appointed to execute the Laws; the public revenues will be squandered on unworthy men; and the rights of the citizen will be violated or disregarded."[99]

We look around us and we watch as our beloved United States of America crumbles. Our elected leaders act as if it is their goal to spend us into oblivion. The only way to understand their pronouncements and actions is if we consider ourselves a conquered people and the Washington-centered oligarchy as an occupying power. We, the silent majority who labor, innovate, and produce are treated as subservient beasts of burden needed and appreciated

---

[98] You Tube https://www.youtube.com/watch?v=Koi_5o9mTsU 1-26-19

[99] Noah Webster quotes http://www.seekfind.net/NoahWebster.html#.XExrdWl7mM8 1-26-19

more for what can be extorted from us than for who we are. Samuel Adams once said, "No people will tamely surrender their Liberties, nor can any be easily subdued, when knowledge is diffused and Virtue is preserved. On the Contrary, when People are universally ignorant, and debauched in their Manners, they will sink under their own weight without the Aid of foreign Invaders."[100]

It is no wonder that we see such a sorry collection of second-rate scoundrels prancing about on the stage of power. They sell their snake oil of class warfare indoctrinating their victims to be needy and then promising to fill their gnawing need with loot legally taken from others. This immoral process breeds a population without the virtue of self-reliance or the honor of being independent. The soul sapping addiction to eternal government support leads to a nation neither adapted to nor deserving of liberty. When a birthright has been sold for a bowl of stew it cannot be regained by demanding more. Thomas Jefferson said, "Dependence begets subservience and venality, suffocates the germ of virtue, and prepares fit tools for the designs of ambition."[101]

---

[100] Quotes on Liberty and Virtue
http://www.liberty1.org/virtue.htm 1-26-19
[101] Ibid.

We the present day guardians of America must stand before the tsunami of anti-education that leads our nation away from virtue and into unrighteousness. We must serve as examples working to earn what we receive and refusing to either play the victim or accept the self-imposed victim-hood of those who seek to expropriate the fruit of someone else's labor. We must stand for righteousness or we will fall before the juggernaut of socialism's final assault upon the land of the free and the home of the brave.

In the coming election we must choose wisely. We must find someone who is virtuous and who adheres to the principles of constitutionally limited government which alone can protect personal liberty, individual freedom, and economic opportunity. Samuel Adams instructed us in this basic truth, "Neither the wisest constitution nor the wisest laws will secure the liberty and happiness of a people whose manners are universally corrupt. He therefore is the truest friend of the liberty of his country who tries most to promote its virtue, and who, so far as his power and influence extend, will not suffer a man to be chosen onto any office of power and trust who is not a wise and virtuous man."[102]

---

[102] Ibid.

Douglas MacArthur warned us, "History fails to record a single precedent in which nations subject to moral decay have not passed into political and economic decline. There has been either a spiritual awakening to overcome the moral lapse, or a progressive deterioration leading to ultimate national disaster."[103]

Finally, looking to the ultimate source of wisdom Proverbs 14:34 tells us, "Righteousness exalts a nation, but sin *is* a reproach to any people."[104]

---

[103] Ibid.
[104] Bible Gateway https://www.biblegateway.com/passage/?search=Proverbs+14%3A34&version=NKJV 1-26-19

Reflection Seventeen

The Joy of the Lord is My Strength

As predicted numerous times in the History of the Future, the Progressive Republican could not defeat the Progressive Democrat. Why would people want a shadow when they can have the real thing?

It was a hard choice to endorse the Progressive Romney, but I felt that the stakes were so high it was worth the effort. As I said repeatedly he might have driven us to the poor house a little bit slower. Instead we have a triumphant President Obama and the Chicago Outfit he represents sitting astride the prostrate body politic. The last four years will be but a prelude to the horrendous destruction these looters will do to the American Experiment in the next four. And given their obvious ability to lead their army of useful idiots, takers, and corrupt city political machines to electoral victory we should probably brace ourselves for President Biden in 2016.

The perpetually re-elected establishment rigidly controls the entrenched two party system, which conveniently calls itself

Democrat and Republican. They are two sides of the same coin, and two wings on the same bird of prey. They both represent the Progressive central-planners who believe government is the answer when we know it is the problem. No matter which side wins the government grows and devours more of the nation's output and its wealth. The election results ratify the electoral majorities' union with the statists. It also points to:

- the permanent establishment of Obamacare
- the probable capture of the Supreme Court
- the loss through re-interpretation of our rights
- the full implementation of the Cloward/Piven Strategy with massive debt , borrowing, and inflation
- the expansion of rule by decree
- the continued and expanded humiliation of America in international affairs
- the end of the American experiment in limited government, personal liberty and economic freedom as we have known it

As alarming as all this sounds do not despair, God did not leave us nor forsake us.[105] First of all He gave us plenty of warning. This author and many others repeatedly predicted an Obama win. As I stated numerous times, the Chicago Machine doesn't lose elections. Also our hope is not in the hand of man. Man didn't give us the peace that passes all understanding and he can't take it away. God gave us His Word which is always our refuge and our fortress.

He told us:

- A thousand may fall at your side, and ten thousand at your right hand; b*ut* it shall not come near you.[106]
- Do Not sorrow, for the joy of the Lord is your strength[107]
- Rejoice in the Lord always. Again I will say, rejoice! Let your gentleness be known to all men. The Lord *is* at hand. Be anxious for nothing, but in everything by prayer and supplication, with thanksgiving, let your requests be made known to God; and the peace of

---

[105] Bible Gateway https://www.biblegateway.com/passage/?search=hebrews%2013:5&version=NKJV 1-26-19

[106] Bible Gateway https://www.biblegateway.com/passage/?search=Psalm%2091&version=NKJV 1-26-19

[107] Bible Gateway https://www.biblegateway.com/passage/?search=Nehemiah%208:10&version=NKJV 1-26-19

God, which surpasses all understanding, will guard your hearts and minds through Christ Jesus.[108]

- God is our refuge and strength, a very present help in trouble. Therefore we will not fear...[109]
- If you confess with your mouth the Lord Jesus and believe in your heart that God has raised Him from the dead, you will be saved. For with the heart one believes unto righteousness, and with the mouth confession is made unto salvation. For the Scripture says, "Whoever believes on Him will not be put to shame."[110]

That is why I can face this morning with joy in my heart and hope in my spirit for I know who my Savior is and I know what He has promised me. Build your life upon the Rock that doesn't roll and when the wind and waves beat against you, you shall not fall.[111]

---

[108] Bible Gateway https://www.biblegateway.com/passage/?search=Phillipians%204&version=NKJV 1-26-19

[109] Bible Gateway https://www.biblegateway.com/passage/?search=psalm%2046&version=NKJV 1-26-19

[110] Bible Gateway https://www.biblegateway.com/passage/?search=Roamns%2010:9-13&version=NKJV 1-26-19

[111] Bible Gateway https://www.biblegateway.com/passage/?search=matthew%207:24-27&version=NKJV 1-26-19

God's Word tells us not to put our trust in leaders whose plans are of this world.[112] Don't look for utopia here. Don't keep your treasure in the world where rust destroys and time forgets instead keep your treasure with God.[113] He promises us that if we draw near to Him He will draw near to us, and that if we humble ourselves before Him He will lift us up.[114]

So don't despair. Don't let the passing victory of the evil steal your joy because if the devil can't steal your joy he can't keep your stuff.[115] And remember, weeping may endure for a night, but joy comes in the morning.[116] Trust God, praise Jesus, and remember: the hope of the righteous will be gladness, but the expectation of the wicked will perish.[117] The plans of the wicked may flourish but they will also wither like the

---

[112] Bible Gateway https://www.biblegateway.com/passage/?search=psalm%20146&version=NKJV 1-26-19

[113] Bible Gateway https://www.biblegateway.com/passage/?search=matthew%206:19-20&version=NKJV 1-26-19

[114] Bible Gateway https://www.biblegateway.com/passage/?search=james%204&version=NKJV 1-26-19

[115] Ministry Helps https://www.ministryhelps.com/if-satan-cant-steal-your-joy-jerry-savelle-p-415.html 1-26-19

[116] Bible Gateway https://www.biblegateway.com/passage/?search=psalm%2030&version=NKJV 1-26-19

[117] Bible Gateway https://www.biblegateway.com/passage/?search=proverbs%2010:28&version=NKJV 1-26-19

flower in the field.[118,119] Trials and tribulations come upon us so that we may grow and persecution was also promised to those who believe along with a way of escape.[120,121,122]

May the God of hope fill you with all joy and peace in believing that you may abound in hope by the power of the Holy Spirit.[123]

Keep the faith, keep the peace, we shall overcome.

---

118 Bible Gateway https://www.biblegateway.com/passage/?search=psalm%2092:7&version=NKJV 1-26-19

119 Bible Gateway https://www.biblegateway.com/passage/?search=james%201&version=NKJV 1-26-19

120 Bible Gateway https://www.biblegateway.com/passage/?search=james%201&version=NKJV 1-26-19

121 Bible Gateway https://www.biblegateway.com/passage/?search=matthew%2010:16-23&version=NKJV 1-26-19

122 Bible Gateway https://www.biblegateway.com/passage/?search=matthew%2010:16-23&version=NKJV 1-26-19

123 Bible Gateway https://www.biblegateway.com/passage/?search=Romans%2015:13&version=NKJV 1-26-19

Reflection Eighteen

The Meaning of The Book of Revelation

A twisted mess of conflicting desires. We want what we want until we get it than we wonder why we wanted it to begin with. So often the wanting is much more fulfilling than the getting because the having is always transitory and the losing is inevitable.

Does that about sum up your experience in the world? It does mine until I met Jesus and committed my life to Him. The answer never quite fit the question. Or was it that the question never quite fit the answer. Either way I always ended up half way home half of the time standing on a cold corner waiting to die alone.

I was always asking, "What's it all about?" Everything seemed so senseless. You work hard all your life and then you die with no U-Haul behind the hearse and no pockets in the shroud. As they used to say in the old neighborhood, "Life's a bitch and then you die."

Once I gave my life to Jesus things changed. Hope was birthed in my life and joy filled my heart. Along the way I found two things that didn't fit the mold of the having not fulfilling the expectation of the wanting. Giving my life to Jesus has proven to be much more than I ever could have expected. And the gift of my wife and the life we have together in Christ grows deeper each day and is better than I ever dreamed possible.

But as to the "What's it all about?" question God did not leave us without an answer. Many seek it in the Book of Revelation. I have found it there and I want to share it with all who can receive it.

In the Sci-Fi classic "A Hitchhiker's Guide to the Galaxy," the mice ask the ultimate question, "What is the meaning to life, the universe, and everything?" Although an enormous supercomputer named Deep Thought over a period of 7.5 million years eventually comes up with the answer, "42" it somehow leaves everyone a bit unsatisfied.

In real life there is an answer to this ultimate question. His name is Jesus.

It is only through my hope in Him that I can walk through this hopeless world. It is only through my joy in Him that I can face the sorrow of knowing that everything in this world that isn't in Him is meaningless. Life in this world is a race around a circle looking for a point. You're young forever until you're old. Almost everyone says, "If I would have known I was going to live this long I would have taken better care of myself" but few ever do even after they know this truth. The young disregard the old and the old disrespect the young. One hand washes another yet neither hand is ever clean.

The religions of this world seek to make us gods. The religion of God seeks to make us Gods'. We cannot possess that which we do not have and that which does not have us seeks to possess us. We enter this world lost and God wants us to find Him so that we can find ourselves in Him. What is the sound of one hand clapping? It is the sound of fingers slapping the heel of our hand. What is the answer to the unanswerable question? It's found in my exegesis of the entire book of Revelation in one sentence.

Jesus is God, God wins in the end, and no matter how bad it gets we should pray, "Even so come Lord Jesus."

There you go. That's it. In other words, "Know Jesus and know peace or, no Jesus and no peace. Every one of us gets to choose for ourselves and in the perfect economy of God through His perfect justice each of us gets what we choose.

Reflection Nineteen

Third Temple Revealed

Do you think we're living in the End Times?

If you spend much time with Evangelical Christians you're bound to be asked this question. Perhaps, more times than you'll be able to remember. I know I have.

Those who believe that the Revelation of John found in the New Testament foretells future evets are constantly looking for signs that the End Times have begun. They're always on the lookout for the birth of the Red Heifer, the discovery of the Ark of the Covenant, and the building of the Third Temple.

News flashes from around the world:

1. The writer of the Book of Hebrews in the New Testament tells us that the end times were already upon us back in the first century when he said, "God, who at various times and in various ways spoke in time past to the fathers by the prophets, has *in these last days* spoken to us by His Son..."

2. The Temple Institute in Jerusalem announced in September of 2018 that the first red heifer born in Israel in 2,000 years "was certified by a board of rabbis as fulfilling all the Biblical requirements."[124]

3. According to the Smithsonian.com the Ark of the Covenant may not have been lost at all. "Through the centuries, Ethiopian Christians have claimed that the ark rests in a chapel in the small town of Aksum, in their country's northern highlands. It arrived nearly 3,000 years ago, they say, and has been guarded by a succession of virgin monks who, once anointed, are forbidden to set foot outside the chapel grounds until they die."[125]

And there are scholars who agree with the Ethiopian Christians. "While the idea that the Ark was taken to Ethiopia is not new there has been renewed interest after evidence was unearthed by the Bible Archaeology, Search & Exploration Institute (BASE). In a blog post on the organization's website it said: "As unusual as this may sound, the BASE team has uncovered compelling evidence that the Ark may well have been spirited up the Nile River to an eventual

---

[124] Breaking Israel News https://www.breakingisraelnews.com/113476/temple-institute-certifies-red-heifer/ 1-26-19

[125] Smithsonian https://www.smithsonianmag.com/travel/keepers-of-the-lost-ark-179998820/ 1-26-19

resting place in the remote highlands of ancient Kush–modern-day Ethiopia.

According to their research the Ark was taken out of the Temple Mount in Jerusalem during the reign of Manasseh where it was first taken to a Jewish colony on Elephantine Island in Egypt.

After that it is thought it was taken down the Nile to Lake Tana in Ethiopia and in particular Tana Kirkos Island, which is considered to be a holy island only populated by Christian monks."

4. And in this article I will reveal the location of the Third Temple.

Let me digress:

When I gave my life to Christ and was born-again into a new life I was an alcoholic drug addict.

I'd never thought that was a bad or unusual thing, either before I was born-again or immediately afterward. Let me explain. You see I thought everyone was an alcoholic drug addict except of course for those bland bobble-heads I called squares or citizens and they meant no more to me than the gravel under my feet. Everyone who was anyone in my life was someone who either helped me get alcohol and drugs or enjoyed them with me.

I didn't think there was anything wrong with using and abusing alcohol and drugs because where I came from everyone did. At least everyone I knew or interacted with. The local priest had his own stool at a local bar and was famous for his capacity to drink people under the table. The pastor of the church my parents attempted to make me attend was a notorious drunk. I knew police officers who got high and arrested people just to seize their drugs. I sat in police cars drinking with on duty officers. My best connection for weed was a Chicago police captain. In my neighborhood teachers, judges, doctors, everyone self-medicated.

I figured the only reason drugs were illegal was because the government had to throw a bone to the mob when they made alcohol legal. And besides in my mind the government made more money running people through the system then they would if they just taxed drug sales. I figured the presidents and others running the country got high they just had the real good stuff.

After I was born-again I was consumed with reading the Bible. As much as possible that was all I did. I would walk around my house reading the Bible drinking whiskey while chain-smoking cigarettes and joints. I just figured I was getting a spiritual high to augment my religious devotion to a self-medicated continuous life buzzzzzzzzzzzzzzz.

It was beautiful.

Then I ran headfirst into I Corinthians 3:16-17, "Do you not know that you are the temple of God and that the Spirit of God dwells in you? If anyone defiles the temple of God, God will destroy him. For the temple of God is holy, which temple you are."[126]

This brought me up short. "I'm the temple of God!" I thought. Looking at the eight ounce tumbler of whiskey in one hand and the cigarette in the other I thought, "What am I doing?"

Right there and right then I set down that glass of whiskey, put out that cigarette looked at the bag of weed lying next to my hands on the desk and gave them up. That was it. No withdrawals. No regrets. God did all the heavy lifting and He made me clean.

Since that day I've never been drawn off course by anyone wondering about when the Third Temple was going to be built because God makes it clear that we are the temple of God. In I Corinthians 3:16-17 He says it straight out, "you are the temple of God."[127] And if that wasn't enough there are other references to this fact in the Bible as well.

---

[126] Bible Gateway https://www.biblegateway.com/passage/?search=1+corinthians+3%3A16-17&version=NKJV 1-26-19

[127] Bible Gateway https://www.biblegateway.com/passage/?search=1+corinthians+3%3A16-17&version=NKJV 1-26-19

Such as I Peter 2:4-5, "Coming to Him as to a living stone, rejected indeed by men, but chosen by God and precious, you also, as living stones, are being built up a spiritual house, a holy priesthood, to offer up spiritual sacrifices acceptable to God through Jesus Christ."[128]

What is the Temple besides God's house? What is it for? It is where the priests offered sacrifices. In the new world, the New Earth[129] we inhabit when we become a new creation[130] the sacrifices are spiritual and they are offered up in God's house, His Holy Temple, which temple we are.[131]

Secret revealed:

Where is the Third Temple? It is right here right now ... it is the body of Christ made up of all believers collectively and individually.[132]

So don't be drawn off base looking for that which has been revealed. Our Father God calls every Christian to be Christ to the world around us. To see with His eyes, hear with

---

[128] Bible Gateway https://www.biblegateway.com/passage/?search=1+peter+2%3A4-5&version=NKJV 1-26-19
[129] Bible Gateway https://www.biblegateway.com/passage/?search=revelation+21%3A1&version=NKJV 1-26-19
[130] Bible Gateway https://www.biblegateway.com/passage/?search=2+CORINTHIANS+5%3A17&version=NKJV 1-26-19
[131] Bible Gateway https://www.biblegateway.com/passage/?search=1+corinthians+3%3A16-17&version=NKJV 1-26-19
[132] Bible Gateway

His ears, touch with His hands, and love with His heart. He told us that we will do the same kind of works He did while He walked among us only greater. So let's not waste our time navel gazing into a reflecting glass of superimposed meanings when Revelation tells us clearly; Jesus is God, God wins in the end, and no matter how bad it gets we should pray, "Even so come Lord Jesus."[133]

[133] Bible Gateway https://www.biblegateway.com/passage/?search=revelation+22%3A20&version=NKJV 1-26-19

Reflection Twenty

Vote For God's Candidate

Election Day 2018 and everything is on the line. At least as far as the direction this country is going to take America First or Globalism, capitalism or socialism. Tune in to any one of the talking heads that litter the airwaves and this is it. This is the BIG one.

As a political science teacher I always tell my students don't let anyone indoctrinate you. Don't let anyone blindly lead you into supporting something you may really disagree with if you knew more. Study the candidates. Study the issues. And then make an informed decision. I also add one more step. Ask God who you should vote for.

One side says if the other side wins they'll make America miserable again. They'll put the brakes on an economy ready to go in orbit, erase the border, and unleash the mob.

The other side says if their opponents win they'll gut social security, close the hospitals, keep illegal children in cages, and continue to confirm judges who will stop common sense gun control and generally bring back slavery.

It's all a soap opera. Yes, it makes sense here in a world ruled by sense knowledge. Yes, it's important who wins here and now but what about in eternity? Ten billion years from now will it make much difference if you were a diehard red or a fanatic blue?

I'm not trying to discourage any one from voting. We should all do our civic duty. We should all study the issues and then vote our conscious. As a pastor I've always counselled vote for God's candidate. Vote for the one who stands up for the things of God. And remember a vote for the lesser of two evils is still voting for evil.

These things intrude upon us from a world that doesn't want to take no. It bombards us 24/7 from TV, radio, and even our phones. The voices and the images fill social media, the wall-to-wall news spigots, and anywhere else anyone might care to look.

Being a history junky and a politicalholic I have battled my entire life to get my mind right. I can easily become obsessed with the History of the Future or current events as some people call it. Until I was thirty years old that was all I had. I only believed in what I could see, touch, and feel. I was ruled by sense knowledge.

But then praise God I met Jesus. He'd been there all along just waiting for me to notice Him. Once I did I realized there was no one else I needed to know. It's like the Bible. Once I realized it is God's Word, His revelation to humanity, the operator's manual for the planet earth I realized that it was the most important book in the world. And as a readaholic that's saying something.

So this morning I wake up on what might be the most important election day of my life and what do I find?

Well, I woke up this morning with my mind, stayin' on Jesus.[134]

Casting Crowns describes and defines our situation well in their hit song *Jesus Friend of Sinners*:[135]

First they aptly describe our current situation:

Jesus, friend of sinners, we have strayed so far away.
We cut down people in your name but the sword was never ours to swing. Jesus, friend of sinners, the truth's become so hard to see The world is on their way to You but they're tripping over me. Always looking around but

[134] Maves Staples Lyrics https://www.azlyrics.com/lyrics/mavisstaples/wokeupthismorningwithmymindonjesus.html 1-26-19

[135] Casting Crowns Lyrics https://www.azlyrics.com/lyrics/castingcrowns/jesusfriendofsinners.html 1-26-19

never looking up I'm so double minded. A plank-eyed saint with dirty hands and a heart divided.

Then after more insightful verses that expose who we are and what we're doing they define what we should do with a question:

Nobody knows what we're for only what we're against when we judge the wounded what if we put down our signs crossed over the lines and loved like You did?

Then Casting Crowns offer a prayer:

Oh Jesus, friend of sinners. Open our eyes to the world at the end of our pointing fingers. Let our hearts be led by mercy. Help us reach with open hearts and open doors. Oh Jesus, friend of sinners, break our hearts for what breaks yours.

The inspiration, knowledge, and hope I always gain from Casting Crowns' songs always leads me back to the place they got it all: the Bible.

We find a story in the Word of God:[136]

The religion scholars and Pharisees led in a woman who had been caught in an act of adultery. They stood her in plain sight of everyone and said, "Teacher, this woman was caught red-handed in the act of adultery.

---

[136] Bible Gateway https://www.biblegateway.com/passage/?search=john+8%3A1-11&version=MSG 1-26-19

Moses, in the Law, gives orders to stone such persons. What do you say?" They were trying to trap him into saying something incriminating so they could bring charges against him.

Jesus bent down and wrote with his finger in the dirt. They kept at him, badgering him. He straightened up and said, "The sinless one among you, go first: Throw the stone." Bending down again, he wrote some more in the dirt.

Hearing that, they walked away, one after another, beginning with the oldest. The woman was left alone. Jesus stood up and spoke to her. "Woman, where are they? Does no one condemn you?"

"No one, Master."

"Neither do I," said Jesus. "Go on your way. From now on, don't sin."

We'll never know until we can ask Him in heaven what Jesus wrote that day in the sand. But the Pharisees and scholars were attempting to trap Him by using the commandments He came to fulfill. And he not only fulfilled the old He also gave us a new commandment when He said, "Let me give you a new command: Love one another. In the same way I loved you, you love one another. This is how everyone will recognize that you are my disciples—when they see the love you have for each other."[137]

As we enter the voting booth today remember as important as this is there is something much more important, something of eternal significance.

Another prayer from Casting Crowns might help us focus:

Help us to remember we are all the least of these
Let the memory of Your mercy bring Your people to their knees.

Pray before you vote and listen to God. If you are His; His voice is ever there guiding and leading you into the paths of righteousness. If we do what He tells us to do we'll always make the right choice and remember His guiding will never conflicts with His Word.

May God bless us one and all as we strive to follow Him and may God bless the United States of America.

I believe this applies to every election every time.

---

[137] Bible Gateway https://www.biblegateway.com/passage/?search=John+13%3A34-35+&version=MSG 1-26-19

Reflection Twenty-one

We Wrestle Not Against Flesh and Blood

Watching the recent political theater that our ever more divided country serves up as leadership reminds me that the natural man cannot receive the things of God for they are foolishness to him. The mockery of the late night political hacks masquerading as comedians or of the not even close to being funny Democrat shills haunting SNL reminds us that weeping may endure for a night but joy comes in the morning.

I wonder if someone came forward and said that Nancy Pelosi sexually abused them when they were a minor but they can't remember where, or when, how they got there, how they got home, and everyone they said was a witness denied it ... do you think the Congressional Ethics Committee would investigate it? Would the ABCCBSNBCPBSCNNMSNBC Cartel do wall-to-wall panel discussion about the validity of the claims?

As we watch these show trials staged for no other reason than to destroy the reputation and life of a man who the testimony of all who know him say is impeccable don't lose heart. What the enemy means for evil God can turn to good. When we see what appears to be all of the media from New York to Hollywood piling on don't despair the enemy may come in like a flood but God is well able to lift up a standard just as Moses lifted a serpent in the wilderness. Look with your spiritual eyes and see the real battle for we don't wrestle against flesh and blood. We battle against principalities, against powers, against the rulers of the darkness of this age, against spiritual hosts of wickedness in the heavenly places.

We'll never have the strength to stand for what's right until we hit our knees. Faith is the answer and prayer is the key. Forget about the unfairness of it for the fallen world is inherently unfair. Take your eyes off the here and now and get a view of eternity. All of this will pass away. Remember God not only wins in the end He's won already. Stop living in the world. Jesus said we must be born again born from above. If we confess Him as Lord if we believe God has raised Him from the dead we will be saved. The moment we do that we enter into His kingdom. We die to this world and we're born into the new heaven and the new earth. And we've done all the dying we'll ever do. Our body will stop one day but we'll live for all eternity in Him.

While it may be entertaining and it may make a world of difference here and now all this back and forth between one side and another is merely man re-arranging the deck chairs on the Titanic. Looking back did it make any difference which side of the deck someone was standing on? We're they on the left or the right? When the ship went down both sides hit the water.

In a hundred years no one will know who we were. Some descendent may know our name, maybe even where we were born and where we died. But they won't know who we are. In a thousand years no one will even know we were here. In a hundred thousand years America will have been erased from memory. But in an eternity from now we who choose to live in Christ will still be praising Him filled with joy and living hope.

The political and social battles of this life may make good TV, they may give us endless hours of animated conversations, and they'll have an impact on the current course of this fallen world. But remember they aren't what they seem. It isn't about right versus left. It's always about good versus evil, light versus dark, and life versus death. But never fear Christ is here. He has won the war and He has told us that "It is finished."

So accept the victory and stop fighting a battle that's already been won.

Reflection Twenty-two

What is Christmas Without Christ?

What have Frosty the Snowman, roasting chestnuts, hippos, hula hoops, and barking dogs got to do with Christmas?

They may bring warmth to our hearts. They may bring a smile to our lips. Or they may make us groan. Whatever they do to each of us what they all have in common is that they're glued to Christmas like barnacles to the hull of the good ship lollipop. They're the accumulated cultural baggage that increasingly obscures the real meaning of a revolutionary blessed event under the camouflage of a socially acceptable winter break.

The ABCCBSNBCCNNMSNBCPBSNPR Cartel tells us constantly that we now live in a post-Christian America. They exalt in proclaiming the end of Christ's dominant influence on Western Civilization. As a result we've descended from a city on a hill to a modern Sodom and Gomorrah. Our elites call evil good and good evil.

Ever since the nine black-robed masters of America decreed back in 1962 that God was expelled from school we've witnessed the steady degradation of our society. The coarseness and vulgarity we're deluged with on a daily basis was unknown in earlier days. What we call prime time entertainment was once known as pornography. What were abominations and generally accepted as perversions have become the norm while believing them to be against God's Word is now considered some type of mental disorder. The cabal of self-appointed paragons of pomposity that masquerade as educators, politicians, and journalists cap their war against God when they glory in the right of self-interest to sacrifice the lives of the innocent and demand that the government not only endorse it but subsidize it.

As a natural outgrowth of the city of man's war against God that defines America's progressive culture comes the war against Christmas.

Back in the dream time we used to go to Christmas programs at our children's schools and listen to the little darlings sing *The First Noel*, *Oh Little Town of Bethlehem*, and *O Come O Come Emmanuel*. Now we listen to them sing songs in foreign languages, or do beautiful arrangements of sounds that don't even have a meaning intermixed with a few songs about winter, snow, or maybe animals. It may all be PC but it sure doesn't have anything to do with the reason for the season.

Just in case all the tinsel and the twinkling lights have blinded us to what that reason is let me elaborate.

Christmas is all about Jesus the Christ born as a human so that he could bear the sins of the world, die a substitutionary death in our place, rise triumphantly from the grave and ascend into heaven so that we who believe can live in and through Him. That's what it's all about. Christmas must be linked to Easter to have any meaning. I've met people who never realized that the Jesus in the manger on Christmas was the same Jesus who hung on the cross on Good Friday. I did not meet them in the jungles of some remote island but in America with a church on every corner. This is a clear case of Santa with a coke in his hand winning the advertising debate over the Lamb who takes away the sins of the world. It may all be PC but it sure doesn't have anything to do with the reason for the season.

What is Christmas without Christ? It's a worldly hedonistic overly commercialized gift giving/receiving orgasm perpetrated by humanity's enemy to keep us from knowing that Christ came to set us free, to reconcile us to God, and to make a way for us to live as a new creation in a new creation.

Not to be Grinch, let me wish everyone a Merry Christmas. Let's enjoy our family and friends. Let's celebrate our traditions as we remember Jesus is the reason for the season. So let's wake up and smell the frankincense and myrrh for without Christ in Christmas all we have is "mas."

Reflection Twenty-three

What is Righteousness and How Do I Get It?

The first part is easy. Righteousness is the ability to stand in the presence of God as if we'd never sinned. When we stand in righteousness before God the Father it's without any sense of fear, condemnation, or inferiority. We have this righteousness because we are now children of God through Christ and as children we are members of the family and have a rightful place.

Just think of Buckingham Palace as heaven. If you walked up to the gate and said, "Let me in" the guards would turn you away. If Prince Charles walked up and said let me in the guards would open the door and bow as he walked past. It's the same way with heaven. If we show up covered in our sin we will get turned away. If we show up in Christ, as a member of His body the gates will swing open and glory to God we will at last be home.

This was promised to us through the prophet Isaiah long ago, "All your children *shall be* taught by the Lord, and great *shall be* the peace of your children. In righteousness you shall be established; you shall be far from oppression, for you shall not fear; and from terror, for it shall not come near you."[138]

As natural men we have a sin consciousness. We inherently know that we are not worthy to stand in the presence of God. We have knowledge of our own weakness to the sins which so easily overtake us. This has kept us slaves to sin. This consciousness of our own sin and weakness destroys our abilities and short-circuits our ability to live as God intends.

That is why we must be born again. For in our re-birth, our re-creation in Christ we acquire righteousness.[139] Without it we could no more be children of God than an ant could be a man. For without righteousness the Father could take no pleasure in us as His children since we would shrink away from the fire of His love since it would then be the fire of His judgement, for it is the same fire.

This righteousness is the gift of God. It is not something we could have ever earned for ourselves. Before we're born again we were without Christ.[140] We were aliens from the

---

[138] Bible Gateway https://www.biblegateway.com/passage/?search=isaiah+54%3A13-14&version=NKJV 1-26-19

[139] Bible Gateway https://www.biblegateway.com/passage/?search=John+3:7&version=NKJV 1-26-19

[140] Bible Gateway https://www.biblegateway.com/passage/?search=ephesians+2%3A12&version=NKJV 1-26-19

commonwealth of Israel and strangers from the covenants of promise, having no hope and without God in the world. We were bankrupt, sold out to sin, and without the ability to help ourselves.

This is why God laid our sins upon Christ. This is why Christ died upon the cross. He paid the penalty demanded by justice. Sin had to be paid for before a fallen mankind could be re-created and in His death, the substitutionary death of the sinless for the sinful the penalty was paid in full.[141] And not only did Christ pay our penalty He descended into Hell, defeated our advisory stripping of his authority over humanity. Then He rose again to give us the promise of eternal life re-created in union with Him through faith.[142]

In the Old Testament Israel had righteousness reckoned to them but in the new creation it actually becomes our very nature because Christ Himself is our Righteousness.[143]

He is the vine and we are the branches. And since the vine is righteous so are the branches. And so should the fruit of the

---

[141] Bible Gateway https://www.biblegateway.com/passage/?search=II+corinthians+5%3A21&version=NKJV 1-26-19
[142] Bible Gateway https://www.biblegateway.com/passage/?search=II+corinthians+5%3A17&version=NKJV 1-26-19
[143] Bible Gateway https://www.biblegateway.com/passage/?search=I+corinthians+1%3A30&version=NKJV 1-26-19

branches be. So we should produce the fruit of righteousness in this world and be a blessing as we are blessed. And we are able to bear a type of fruit that Christ could not when He walked this earth. He could heal the sick, raise the dead, and calm the storm. But He could not lead people to salvation for He had not yet paid the price. He had not yet opened the way for us to be re-united with God erasing the sin debt of Adam's fall.

So that is righteousness, right standing with God, the ability to stand in God's presence as if we had never sinned. We get it through confessing with our lips that Jesus is Lord and by believing in our heart that God has raised Him from the dead.[144]

And once we have it we are tasked by Christ to share our witness so that all mankind has the opportunity to have it too.[145]

---

[144] Bible Gateway https://www.biblegateway.com/passage/?search=Romans+10%3A9-10%2C+and+13&version=NKJV 1-26-19

[145] Bible Gateway https://www.biblegateway.com/passage/?search=acts+1%3A8&version=NKJV 1-26-19

Reflection Twenty-four

Why is More Important Than How

Does the immensity of creation ever overwhelm you? Does the fact that when you lay your hand on the cold hard surface of a table there is actually more space than matter in the table numb your mind? When you're sitting on a beach letting the sand run through your fingers have you ever reflected on the thought that there are more stars in the universe than there are grains of sand on the earth? Has the image of reality extending as deep through a microscope as it does through a telescope make you grasp for understanding when all you can possibly understand is that you can't understand this immensity at all?

Science tries to explain it all.

Back in the 1890s Albert Abraham Michelson an American physicist known for his work on measuring the speed of light who received the Nobel Prize in Physics, becoming the first American to win the Nobel Prize in a science put it this way, "While it is never safe to affirm that the future of Physical Science has no marvels in store even more astonishing than those of the past, it seems probable that most of the grand underlying principles have been firmly established and that further advances are to be sought chiefly in the rigorous application of these principles to all the phenomena which come under our notice. It is here that the science of measurement shows its importance — where quantitative work is more to be desired than qualitative work. An eminent physicist remarked that the future truths of physical sciences are to be looked for in the sixth place of decimals."[146]

In other words the deepest thinkers came to the conclusion there was nothing new to be discovered in physics. All that remains is more and more precise measurement.

Since then the theories of Special Relativity and Quantum Mechanics have shown us that we know a lot less than we thought we did. I guess it took a genius like Einstein to discover that we aren't as smart as we think we are. And yet most of us who figured that out by about eighth grade continue to listen to these geniuses when they tell us they can figure out everything else.

And while science is pretty good at explaining the "how" of things they always leave out the "Why."

---

[146] Quora https://www.quora.com/Which-19th-century-physicist-famously-said-that-all-that-remained-to-be-done-in-physics-was-compute-effects-to-another-decimal-place 1-26-19

They can tell us there was a BIG BANG (the "Let there be" experience for believers) they even try to tell us how there was BIG BANG, but they never even attempt to tell us why there was BIG BANG.

And to my mind and my heart the why is more important than the how.

Science is great at identifying things. They are passable at explaining things. Yet, when it comes to this ultimate question of why, science never utters a sound.

Look at life. Scientists can identify it. They can quantify it. They have attempted to tell us how it became so diversified. They now even say they can create it. But they never tell us why there is life.

Have you ever wondered why?

Life is the essence of the universe. Life is the ultimate goal and it's the meaning of everything.

The Bible is the why book. It is the operating manual for life. It not only tells us how ... God created everything. It tells us why ... as a dwelling place for the crown of His creation ... humanity.

Why?

In the Old Testament God is specifically called the Father of the nation of Israel (Deut 32:6 ; Isa 63:16 ; 64:8 ; Jeremiah 3:4

Jeremiah 3:19 ; 31:9 ; Mal 1:6 ; 2:10) or the Father of certain individuals (2 Sam 7:14 ; 1 Chron 17:13 ; 22:10 ; 28:6 ; Psalm 68:5 ; 89:26) fifteen times. At times the father imagery is present although the term "Father" is not used (Exod 4:22-23 ; Deut 1:31 ; 8:5 ; 14:1 ; Psalm 103:13 ; Jer 3:22 ; 31:20 ; Hosea 11:1-4 ; Mal 3:17).

In the intertestamental literature the term is also used. In the Apocrypha[147] (Wis 2:16; 14:3; Tob 13:4; Sir 23:1, 4; 51:10); and in the Pseudepigrapha[148] (Jub 1:24; 19:29; 3 Macc 5:7; 6:8).

The teaching of the Fatherhood of God takes a decided turn with Jesus, for "Father" was His favorite term for addressing God. It appears on His lips some sixty-five times in the Synoptic Gospels and over one hundred times in John.

Because of Jesus' use of this metaphor, it is not surprising that the rest of the New Testament also emphasizes the Fatherhood of God. In the Pauline letters God is described as "Father" over forty times. It occurs in blessings (Rom 1:7 ; 1 Cor 1:3), doxologies (Rom 15:6), thanksgivings (2 Cor 1:3 ; 1 Thess 1:2-3), prayers (Col 1:12),

---

[147] International Bible Society https://www.quora.com/Which-19th-century-physicist-famously-said-that-all-that-remained-to-be-done-in-physics-was-compute-effects-to-another-decimal-place 1-26-19

[148] Compelling Truth https://www.compellingtruth.org/Pseudepigrapha.html 1-26-19

exhortations (Eph 5:20), and creeds (1 Cor 8:6 ; Eph 4:6). For Paul this fatherhood is based not so much on God's role in creation but rather on the redemption and reconciliation he has made available in Jesus Christ. This is why Paul refers to "the God and Father of our Lord Jesus Christ" (Rom 15:6 ; 2 Cor 1:3 ; 11:31). It is through the work of Christ that God invites us to call him "*Abba,* Father." It is through Christ that grace and peace have resulted and we have become God's children (Rom 8:12-16 ; 1 Peter 1:3-4 ; 1 John 3:1).

This is not to say that God is male. He is spirit and as such is neither male nor female. It is not to denigrate motherhood. For who among us would desire to live in a world without a mother's love. When God is referred as a father, this is simply the use of a metaphor in which he is likened to a kind and loving father. And if we were to tip our hat to the political correctness of the day by avoiding the metaphor of father as a description and designation for God we would lose sight of the fact that Jesus chose this as His metaphor to address God and that He taught this as the metaphor by which His disciples should address God.[149]

---

[149] Bible Gateway https://www.biblegateway.com/passage/?search=mathew+6%3A9-13&version=NKJV 1-26-19

It also loses sight of the continuity established by the use of this metaphor with those who have called God "Father" over the centuries. These Include the disciples; the earliest congregations (Rom 8:15 ; Gal 4:6); the earliest church councils ("I believe in God the Father Almighty, Maker of heaven and earth "); and Christian churches all over the globe who over the centuries have prayed together "Our Father in heaven, Hallowed be Your name."[150]

Because of God's Fatherhood the heart of the Eternal Father longed for children.[151] This is why He created Adam and Eve and gave them the power to go forth and multiply. Unfortunately they sinned and fell short of the glory of God.[152] There was no way back. They had surrendered their place as God's companion, the gardener of Eden to Satan and were cast out.

But God in His infinite mercy and love made a way back.

He sent Jesus to live a sinless life and then die as the sacrifice, the payment for all our sins so that all who have faith in Him can be

---

[150] Bible Gateway https://www.biblegateway.com/passage/?search=mathew+6%3A9-13&version=NKJV 1-26-19
[151] Billy Graham https://www.biblestudytools.com/dictionaries/bakers-evangelical-dictionary/fatherhood-of-god.html 1-26-19
[152] Bible Gateway https://www.biblegateway.com/passage/?search=genisis+3%3A1-24&version=NKJV 1-26-19

counted as righteous and thus re-united with God.

It's all summed up in this; if you confess with your mouth the Lord Jesus and believe in your heart that God has raised Him from the dead, you will be saved.[153]

We are born lost and rejected, children of sin and children of the devil. If we turn away from the world and accept Jesus as our Savior we are born again and we become children of God in Christ.

This is the why. All of creation is for one reason and that is to bring children to God and fulfill the Father's love that is His heart.

So science may try to tell us how but you see the why is more important than the how.

A short story to highlight the what, the where, and the how:

A scientist says to God, "You're not so much we have figured out how to make life in our laboratories."

God says, "Oh, you have."

The scientist, swelling with pride then says, "Come on let's have a contest and see who can make life the quickest and the best."

God smiles and says, "All right."

---

[153] Bible Gateay https://www.biblegateway.com/passage/?search=Romans+10%3A9&version=NKJV 1-26-19

God reaches down and picks up a hand full of dirt and starts molding it gently.

The scientist adds some chemicals to a couple of test tubes and starts mixing them back and forth.

God looks over at the scientist and says, "Hey! Get your own dirt."

From atom to Adam God has done it all. So if you find yourself hung up in the how just remember the why is more important than the how. And if you find yourself questioning God just remember, "He's the Father that's why."

Reflection Twenty-five

Why Worry When You Can Pray

I am often asked, "How can you stay focused so intently upon the situations and circumstances surrounding America's current condition of managed decline without succumbing to the mind-chilling depression it warrants?"

How can I watch with the contextual awareness of an Historian the seemingly unstoppable advance of the progressives in their quest to re-build America in their own image without falling victim to the lure of apathy and the thrill of the games?

What is it that allows me to gaze daily at the man-caused disasters which befall us as we morph from our nation to the Obamanation without embracing the nihilism so common to the citizens of falling empires?

There is one common solution to these apparent paradoxes. There is one answer to these discomforting questions. Because there is one name that stands above all nations, all circumstances, and all names and that name is Jesus.

If it wasn't for my rock solid faith in Jesus I would despair. If it wasn't for my faith in Jesus I would turn away from the shame of our surrender, the enormity of our decline and the potential of our looming defeat. As a believer in limited government, personal liberty and economic freedom without Jesus I would give-up. I would look at the reality of our situation and admit the subjugation of my nation to this band of looting utopians who have gathered the reins of power and are leading us like sheep to the slaughter into a dystopian future of unlimited government, personal servitude, and a centrally-planned economy.

However, I do have Jesus as my personal Savior. I confess Him as my Lord and Savior. I believe that God has raised Him from the dead, and that He will come again.

Yes, I follow current events, the History of the Future,[154] like a housewife follows her people on any other soap opera. For years I tuned in every day to see what new perils Lady Liberty faces, and what dastardly deeds Simon Lagree Obama[155] would perpetrate upon the chained and restrained citizens who watch helplessly as their nation floats on an ice flow of freedom constantly melting beneath them. Yet just like those readers of

---

[154] Drrobertowens.com
[155] Cliff's Notes https://www.cliffsnotes.com/literature/u/uncle-toms-cabin/character-analysis/simon-legree 1-26-19

Uncle Tom's cabin so long ago I have my Tom. I have my joy and the lifter of my head. I have Jesus. So I know that no matter what happens here and no matter what may happen to me or mine He will be my reward.

The followers of some other religion who say they are a religion of peace may have declared war upon us. They have adopted a policy of convert or die. However I know that Jesus has already won the war. I know that He has already died for me and though this body may perish He has already done all the dying I will ever have to do.

It was not always this way. Yes, I have always been obsessed with current events. Yes, I have always studied History, economics, and political science. Yes, I have always been aware of the context and the goal of the Progressive horde. However there was a time when I didn't have this hope that lives inside of me. There was a time when the thought of being a pawn in a rigged game, being the citizen of an occupied nation sold by uninformed voters to demagogues intent upon the subversion of the Constitution drove me to despair. Watching the incremental surrender caused me to embrace a philosophy of militant apathy. I didn't care and I couldn't stand anyone who did.

This led to a hollowness that made any success or pleasure I experienced seem futile and merely a diversion. I was an atheist. I didn't believe in God. I didn't believe in spirits. All I believed in was what I could see, and all I could see was the decay of something once promising: the selling of the land of the free and the home of the brave for a bowl of pottage called entitlement. At the age of thirty I had reached my limit. I was convinced nothing meant anything. I was sure that my nation on its way to freedom had turned around and looked longingly at the chains of tyranny they had broken and was turning before my eyes into a pillar of salt. It seemed no one could read the handwriting on the wall, and I was playing the fiddle while Rome burned.

There came a time when I was saying to myself over and over, "I've got to try something, I've got to try something." I was a drug addict, an alcoholic, and I thought if I could just find a better high or a smoother whiskey all my anxieties would disappear. No matter what I tried it didn't work. The rotting stench of decay still filled my mind. I couldn't take my eyes off the slow motion train wreck that has been America's path. I was thinking the unthinkable and wondering if there was any reason to go on? I didn't believe in an afterlife. I believed that here was all there was. So I thought if I wasn't here the sorrow would stop. Yet something within me still clutched at straws and kept saying, "I've got to try something, I've got to try something."

Then one day as I went about my work saying this to myself over and over, I heard someone say, "Why don't you try Jesus." As a devout believer in Militant Apathy and a devout non-believer in everything else I turned to follow my regular pattern of smashing in the face of anyone foolish enough to mention Jesus to me, and no one was there. I was in a church for a secular reason at the time and there was no one else in the entire building. I know because I looked. I had distinctly heard an answer to my perennial question, "Why don't you try Jesus" yet I knew no one else was there.

As an atheist who didn't believe in anything except the visible, that was, to say the least, disconcerting. I started attending that church the next week. It was Christian church. I knew from my youth the Christianity, which I had rejected in that same youth, was built upon the Bible so I started reading.

I read Mathew, Mark, Luke, and john. By the time I finished John I knew I had to make a decision. All of this was either true or it was false. If it was false it was just another lie in a world filled with lies. But if it was true it was the most important truth in the world. I knew from my study of History that many of the early followers of Jesus including Matthew, Mark, Luke, and John were killed because of their faith. I also knew that each of them had been given the opportunity to reject Jesus, admit what they had written and what they preached was lies and live, or they could affirm the truth of what they said and die. I knew they had all chosen death rather than say it was a lie.

Then I reasoned, if this story, this good news about a God who became flesh, paid the price of all sin by dying a sinless death upon a cross, and who purchased our everlasting life by defeating death rising from the grave was a lie they would have known it since they wrote it. They would have known there was no Savior, no salvation, and that their death would have been final. They would have known all this, and they would have chosen life over death. They didn't. They chose death in this life, because they believed in a life after this life: the life their writing told us about.

At that moment I asked Jesus to be my Savior. Suddenly a light burst forth in my being that has never gone out. A joy replaced the sadness. Hope replaced depression as I chose life over death, and I have spent every day since then trying to live for Him because He chose to live for me. Since that day it has never been about who I am but about what He's done and not about what I've done but about who He is.[156]

Jesus Christ my Lord and Savior.

If you are overwhelmed by the calamity which is looming in our future, by the soul crushing sadness of living as citizens of a city on the hill that is committing suicide before our eyes..........

Turn your eyes upon Jesus Look full in His wonderful face, and the things of earth will grow strangely dim,
In the light of His glory and grace.[157]

Now the change that people voted for in 2008 has collided into the change people voted for in 2016 and as that wanders down the halls of History Ad infinitum .... why worry when you can pray.... ;--)

Keep the faith. Keep the peace.

We shall overcome in Him, through Him, and for Him.

---

[156] Casting Crowns Lyrics https://www.azlyrics.com/lyrics/castingcrowns/whoami.html 1-26-19

[157] Timeless Truths https://library.timelesstruths.org/music/Turn_Your_Eyes_upon_Jesus/ 1-26-19

Conclusion

This whole living a life of faith is really a matter of living in the Spirit of Christ.

When I first gave my life to Christ I gave myself over to the study of the Word of God. I saw things like turning the other cheek[158] and returning blessings for evil[159] as guidance about how to live. Reading it was one thing. Trying to implement it in my every day walking around in the world life was another. It felt like trying to learn how to walk backwards. It was counterintuitive to say the least when compared to how I had been raised. It bore little resemblance to the lives I saw people living around me.

It just didn't make any sense. At least not until I began trying it on for size. Then I realized that life as the world taught me to live it was a zombie life. I was more a dead man walking through a world filled with pain, tears, and confusion than anything else. Once I opened myself up to trying to do it God's way I found out what life is really like.

---

[158] Bible Gateway https://www.biblegateway.com/passage/?search=matthew+5%3A39&version=NKJV 1-27-19

[159] Bible Gateway https://www.biblegateway.com/passage/?search=1+peter+3%3A8-9&version=NKJV 1-27-19

Once again this is expressed as well as it ever could be by Eugene Peterson in Galatian 6:16-26 of *The Message*,[160]

My counsel is this: Live freely, animated and motivated by God's Spirit. Then you won't feed the compulsions of selfishness. For there is a root of sinful self-interest in us that is at odds with a free spirit, just as the free spirit is incompatible with selfishness. These two ways of life are antithetical, so that you cannot live at times one way and at times another way according to how you feel on any given day. Why don't you choose to be led by the Spirit and so escape the erratic compulsions of a law-dominated existence?

It is obvious what kind of life develops out of trying to get your own way all the time: repetitive, loveless, cheap sex; a stinking accumulation of mental and emotional garbage; frenzied and joyless grabs for happiness; trinket gods; magic-show religion; paranoid loneliness; cutthroat competition; all-consuming-yet-never-satisfied wants; a brutal temper; an impotence to love or be loved; divided homes and divided lives; small-minded and lopsided pursuits; the vicious habit of depersonalizing everyone into a rival; uncontrolled and uncontrollable addictions; ugly parodies of community. I could go on.

---

[160] The Message http://messagebible.com/ 1-27-19

This isn't the first time I have warned you, you know. If you use your freedom this way, you will not inherit God's kingdom.

But what happens when we live God's way? He brings gifts into our lives, much the same way that fruit appears in an orchard—things like affection for others, exuberance about life, serenity. We develop a willingness to stick with things, a sense of compassion in the heart, and a conviction that a basic holiness permeates things and people. We find ourselves involved in loyal commitments, not needing to force our way in life, able to marshal and direct our energies wisely.

Legalism is helpless in bringing this about; it only gets in the way. Among those who belong to Christ, everything connected with getting our own way and mindlessly responding to what everyone else calls necessities is killed off for good—crucified.

Since this is the kind of life we have chosen, the life of the Spirit, let us make sure that we do not just hold it as an idea in our heads or a sentiment in our hearts, but work out its implications in every detail of our lives. That means we will not compare ourselves with each other as if one of us were better and another worse. We have far more interesting things to do with our lives. Each of us is an original.[161]

And once again all I can say to that is:
Amen and Amen.

Robert R. Owens

[161] Bible Gateway https://www.biblegateway.com/passage/?search=galatians+5%3A16-26&version=MSG 1-27-19

Made in the USA
Monee, IL
07 November 2020

46936122R00085